ESSENTIAL LEADERSHIP SKILLS AND CONFLICT RESOLUTION STRATEGIES FOR MANAGERS

(2 Books in 1)

Proven Techniques to Manage Teams, Inspire
Performance, and Resolve Workplace Challenges

AMBER PRESTON

Table of Contents

Leadership Skills for Managers
7 Practical Skills to Master the Art of Communication, Enhance Decision-Making Capabilities, and Inspire High-Performing Teams

Conflict Resolution Guidebook for Managers
Essential Skills for Preventing, Managing, and Resolving Conflict in the Workplace

Leadership Skills for Managers

7 PRACTICAL SKILLS TO MASTER THE ART OF COMMUNICATION, ENHANCE DECISION-MAKING CAPABILITIES, AND INSPIRE HIGH-PERFORMING TEAMS

Introduction

So, you've landed a management role. Congrats! It's exciting, but let's be real—it's also scary as heck. You're suddenly dealing with all these new challenges, like figuring out team dynamics, making tough calls, and trying to establish yourself as a leader. Sound about right?

If you're nodding your head, you're not alone. Most managers have moments where they question their ability to lead effectively. Maybe you've had a hard time getting your vision across, or you've struggled with motivating your team. Perhaps you've even wondered if you're cut out for this whole leadership thing.

Here's the thing: Doubts and challenges are just part of the deal when it comes to leadership. But the good news? You don't have to go it alone. This book is here to guide you, support you, and give you the tools you need as you step into becoming a confident, capable, and inspiring leader.

So, what brought you here? Maybe you're brand new to management and want to start strong. Or perhaps you've been doing this for a while, but you're looking to sharpen your skills and keep up with the changing workplace. Wherever you're at, if you're looking for practical strategies to level up your leadership, you're in the right place.

In this book, you'll find insights and strategies to help you

- communicate effectively and create a culture of trust and transparency
- develop a clear vision and think strategically to drive results
- make smart, empowered decisions that benefit your team and your organization
- inspire and motivate your employees to be their best
- delegate well and foster a sense of ownership and independence in your team
- lead with integrity and compassion, even when things get tough
- create an inclusive, diverse workplace where everyone feels valued and respected
- adapt your leadership approach for remote and hybrid work situations

And that's not all. By the time you finish this book, you'll have a solid set of leadership strategies, *and* you'll have a better understanding of your own unique leadership style and potential. You'll feel more confident navigating the ins and outs of management, and you'll be ready to create a positive, productive, and fulfilling work environment for you and your team.

Now, you might be thinking, *Am I really ready for this? How do I even assess my current leadership skills?* We've got you. Below is access to a free leadership self-assessment that will help you identify your strengths and areas for growth. This assessment is a great starting point for your leadership development journey, and it will help you get the most out of the strategies and insights in this book.

For the free leadership self-assessment, scan the QR code or click here!

Before we jump in, let's acknowledge that leadership isn't a one-and-done thing. It's an ongoing journey of learning, growing, and discovering more about yourself. The strategies and insights in this book aren't a magic solution that will make you a perfect leader overnight. They're tools and frameworks that, when you use them consistently and intentionally, will help you become the best leader you can be.

Leadership expert John C. Maxwell (n.d.) said, "A leader is one who knows the way, goes the way, and shows the way." By picking up this book, you're already taking the first step in knowing the way. Now, it's time to go the way and show the way.

So, whether you're a brand new manager or a seasoned leader looking to take your skills up a notch, this book is your invitation to start a transformative leadership journey. Get ready to tap into your full potential, inspire your team, and make a real impact in your organization and beyond.

ONE

Understanding Your Role as a Leader

A leader is one who knows the way, goes the way, and shows the way.

John C. Maxwell

This powerful quote from leadership expert John C. Maxwell encapsulates the essence of what it means to be a leader. As you step into your role as a manager, it's crucial to understand the significance of your position and the impact you can have on your team and organization.

In this chapter, we'll explore what leadership and management mean, why good management matters, and the mindset and qualities that define effective leaders. By the end of this chapter, you'll have a clearer understanding of your role and feel more confident in your ability to lead.

What It Means to Be a Leader

Leadership is a complex and multifaceted concept that can be defined in many ways. At its core, leadership is about influencing, guiding, and inspiring others to achieve a common goal. It's about setting a direction, creating a vision, and empowering people to reach their full potential.

Leadership comes in many shapes and forms. It can be formal, like a managerial position, or informal, like a team member who takes initiative and inspires others through their actions. It can be loud and charismatic or quiet and understated. What matters most is the impact a leader has on their team and the results they achieve.

So, what does it mean to be a manager specifically? A manager is responsible for overseeing and coordinating the work of a team to achieve organizational goals. This involves planning, organizing, staffing, directing, and controlling resources and people.

But being a manager is about more than just assigning tasks and hitting targets. It's about creating a positive work environment, developing your team members, and fostering a culture of trust, collaboration, and continuous improvement. As a manager, you have a direct impact on the engagement, productivity, and well-being of your team.

Managers wear many hats and juggle multiple responsibilities. They're coaches, mentors, problem-solvers, decision-makers, and communicators. They're accountable for the performance and development of their team members, as well as the overall success of their department or function.

To be effective in these roles, managers need a wide range of skills and competencies. These include:

- **Technical skills:** Knowledge and expertise in the specific areas they manage, such as finance, marketing, or operations.
- **Interpersonal skills:** The ability to build and maintain positive relationships with team members, colleagues, and stakeholders.
- **Communication skills:** The ability to clearly and persuasively convey information, expectations, and feedback.
- **Problem-solving skills:** The ability to identify and analyze problems, generate solutions, and make sound decisions.
- **Emotional intelligence:** The ability to understand and manage one's own emotions and the emotions of others.
- **Adaptability:** The ability to flexibly respond to change and uncertainty and to learn and grow from new experiences.

Developing these skills takes time, practice, and a commitment to continuous learning and improvement. As a manager, it's important to actively seek out opportunities to build your skills and knowledge, whether through formal training, mentorship, or on-the-job experience.

The Importance of Good Management

Why does good management matter? Simply put, it's essential for the success and sustainability of any organization. Good management practices lead to:

- increased productivity and efficiency
- higher employee engagement and job satisfaction
- lower turnover and absenteeism
- improved customer satisfaction and loyalty
- better financial performance and profitability

On the flip side, poor management can have devastating consequences. It can lead to low morale, high stress, conflict, and ultimately, organizational failure. As a manager, the buck stops with you. Your actions and decisions have a ripple effect on your team and the broader organization.

Consider the impact of a manager who micromanages their team, constantly checking in and controlling every aspect of their work. This type of management style can stifle creativity, innovation, and autonomy, leading to disengagement and resentment among team members.

On the other hand, a manager who empowers their team, provides clear expectations and feedback, and supports their development can create a positive and productive work environment. This type of management style can lead to higher levels of motivation, commitment, and performance among team members.

Good management also plays a critical role in shaping organizational culture. As a manager, you set the tone and model the behaviors and values that define your team and your organization. If you prioritize transparency, accountability, and respect, your team is more likely to embody those same qualities.

Ultimately, the success of any organization depends on the quality of its management. As a manager, you have the power and responsibility to drive positive change, inspire excellence, and create value for your team, your customers, and your stakeholders.

The Leadership Mindset

To be an effective leader, it's not enough to just know what to do. You also need to have the right mindset. A leadership mindset is a way of thinking and being that enables you to inspire, influence, and achieve results through others.

So, what makes up a leadership mindset? Here are some key elements:

- **Vision:** Having a clear and compelling vision of what you want to achieve and why it matters.
- **Courage:** Being willing to take risks, make tough decisions, and stand up for what you believe in.
- **Empathy:** Being able to understand and connect with others on a human level.
- **Growth:** Continuously learning, adapting, and improving yourself and your team.
- **Accountability:** Taking ownership of your actions and results and holding yourself and others accountable.
- **Service:** Putting the needs of your team and organization before your own.

Developing a leadership mindset is an ongoing process. It requires self-awareness, reflection, and a willingness to step outside your comfort zone. But the payoff is worth it. With the right mindset, you'll be better equipped to navigate challenges, inspire your team, and drive results.

One key aspect of a leadership mindset is a growth mindset. Coined by psychologist Carol Dweck, a growth mindset is the belief that your abilities and intelligence can be developed through hard work, dedication, and perseverance. Leaders with a growth mindset embrace challenges, learn from failure, and continually seek out opportunities to improve and grow.

In contrast, a fixed mindset is the belief that your abilities and intelligence are fixed traits that cannot be changed. Leaders with a fixed mindset avoid challenges, fear failure, and are resistant to feedback and criticism. They may plateau in their development and limit their potential for success.

As a leader, cultivating a growth mindset in yourself and your team can have a powerful impact on performance and innovation. It can create a culture of learning, experimentation, and continuous improvement, where people feel empowered to take risks and push boundaries.

Another important element of a leadership mindset is emotional intelligence. Emotional intelligence is the ability to understand and manage your own emotions and the emotions of others. It includes skills like self-awareness, self-regulation, motivation, empathy, and social skills.

Leaders with high emotional intelligence are better able to build trust, resolve conflicts, and create positive relationships with their team members and stakeholders. They're able to read and respond to the emotional needs of others and to create a supportive and inclusive work environment.

Developing emotional intelligence requires practice and self-reflection. It involves paying attention to your own emotions and reactions and learning to regulate them in healthy and productive ways. It also involves actively listening to others, showing empathy and compassion, and building strong social connections.

Confidence and Leadership

One of the most important qualities of a leader is confidence. Confident leaders inspire trust, build credibility, and create a sense of stability and direction for their teams. They're able to make tough decisions, take calculated risks, and bounce back from setbacks.

But what does confident leadership look like in practice? Here are some key indicators:

- **Decisiveness:** Being able to make clear and timely decisions, even in the face of uncertainty or opposition.
- **Composure:** Staying calm and collected under pressure, and being able to regulate your emotions.
- **Communication:** Being able to articulate your vision and expectations clearly and persuasively.
- **Presence:** Having a commanding and engaging presence that draws people in and inspires them to follow you.
- **Humility:** Being able to admit when you're wrong, learn from your mistakes, and give credit to others.

Of course, building confidence as a leader is easier said than done. Many leaders struggle with self-doubt, impostor syndrome, and other barriers to confidence.

Impostor syndrome, in particular, is a common challenge for leaders. It's the feeling that you're not good enough, that you're a fraud, and that you'll be found out at any moment. Symptoms of impostor syndrome include:

- **Perfectionism:** Setting unrealistic standards for yourself and feeling like a failure when you don't meet them.

- **Overworking:** Putting in long hours and taking on extra projects to prove your worth.
- **Discounting praise:** Downplaying your accomplishments and attributing your success to luck or other external factors.
- **Fear of failure:** Avoiding risks and challenges because you're afraid of failing or looking foolish.

If you're struggling with impostor syndrome, know that you're not alone. Many successful leaders have dealt with these feelings at some point in their careers. The key is to recognize the symptoms and take steps to overcome them.

Here are some strategies for building confidence and combating impostor syndrome:

- **Focus on your strengths:** Identify your unique skills and talents, and play to them in your leadership role.
- **Reframe failure:** See failure as an opportunity to learn and grow rather than a reflection of your worth as a leader.
- **Seek feedback:** Ask for honest and constructive feedback from your team and colleagues, and use it to improve your leadership skills.
- **Practice self-compassion:** Treat yourself with kindness and understanding, and acknowledge that everyone makes mistakes and has areas for growth.

Another way to build confidence as a leader is to focus on your accomplishments and successes. Keep a record of your achievements, both big and small, and refer back to them when you're feeling unsure or down on yourself. Celebrate your wins and the wins of your team, and use them as evidence of your leadership abilities.

It's also important to surround yourself with supportive people who believe in you and your leadership potential. Seek mentors, coaches, and peers who can provide guidance, encouragement, and honest feedback. Build a network of trusted advisors who can help you navigate challenges and celebrate your successes.

Finally, remember that confidence is not about being perfect or having all the answers. It's about being authentic, vulnerable, and willing to learn and grow. As a leader, you don't have to have it all figured out. What matters is that you show up with integrity, empathy, and a commitment to doing your best for your team and your organization.

Leadership Presence

Another key aspect of leadership is presence. Leadership presence is the ability to command attention, inspire confidence, and influence others through physical, emotional, and verbal communication.

Leadership presence is about more than just charisma or stage presence. It's about being authentic, consistent, and purposeful in how you show up as a leader. It's about aligning your words, actions, and values to create a strong and positive impression.

So, what does leadership presence look like in action? Here are some examples:

- A CEO who delivers a powerful and inspiring speech at a company-wide meeting, rallying the team around a new strategy.

- A manager who stays calm and focused during a crisis, providing clear direction and support to their team.
- A team leader who actively listens to their colleagues, asks thoughtful questions, and provides constructive feedback.

Developing leadership presence is a skill that can be learned and practiced over time. Here are some tips for improving your leadership presence:

- **Be self-aware:** Pay attention to how you come across to others, and adjust your behavior and communication style accordingly.
- **Be present:** Give your full attention to the people and situations in front of you, and avoid distractions or multitasking.
- **Be intentional:** Plan and prepare for important interactions or presentations, and think about the impact you want to have.
- **Be authentic:** Be true to yourself and your values, and avoid trying to be someone you're not.
- **Be confident:** Trust in your abilities and expertise, and project a sense of calm and assurance.

One important aspect of leadership presence is nonverbal communication. Your body language, facial expressions, and tone of voice can all convey powerful messages and emotions to others. As a leader, it's important to be aware of your nonverbal cues and to use them intentionally to reinforce your message and build trust and credibility with your team.

For example, maintaining eye contact, using open body language, and speaking with a clear and confident voice can all help to convey authority and engagement. On the other hand, fidgeting, crossing your arms, or speaking in a monotone voice can all undermine your presence and influence.

Another key aspect of leadership presence is emotional intelligence. As we discussed earlier, emotional intelligence is the ability to understand and manage your own emotions and the emotions of others. Leaders with high emotional intelligence are better able to connect with their team members, build trust and rapport, and navigate complex social situations.

To learn more about developing your emotional intelligence, I highly recommend checking out my book *Mastering Emotional Intelligence With Ease.* In it, I dive deeper into the strategies and techniques you can use to build your emotional intelligence skills and become a more effective leader.

Try practicing active listening and empathy to develop your emotional intelligence and leadership presence. When communicating with others, focus on fully understanding their perspective and needs and respond with compassion and respect. Avoid jumping to conclusions or making assumptions, and be willing to admit when you're wrong or need more information.

It's also important to manage your own emotions and reactions, especially in high-pressure or challenging situations. Take deep breaths, stay calm and focused, and avoid letting your emotions get the best of you. Model the behavior and attitudes you want to see in your team, and be consistent in your words and actions.

Wrapping Up

In this chapter, we've laid the foundation for understanding your role as a leader and manager. We've explored what leadership means, why good management matters, and the mindset and qualities that define effective leadership.

We've covered key concepts, including:

- the essence of leadership and management and how they differ
- the importance of good management for organizational success
- the leadership mindset and its components, such as vision, courage, and empathy
- the role of confidence and leadership presence in inspiring and influencing others
- strategies for building confidence and overcoming impostor syndrome

Understanding your role as a leader is the first step in your leadership journey. By recognizing the significance of your position and the impact you can have on your team and organization, you're setting the stage for personal and professional growth.

Equipped with this knowledge, you're now ready to dive deeper into the specific skills and practices that will help you become a more confident, capable, and inspiring leader. In the chapters ahead, we'll explore topics such as communication, vision-setting, decision-making, and team development, providing you with practical tools and insights to take your leadership to the next level.

Remember, leadership is a continuous journey of learning, growing, and adapting. Embrace this opportunity with passion, integrity, and a commitment to excellence, and you'll have the power to make a lasting impact on your team, your organization, and the world.

Case Study: Abigail

Abigail had been working as a software engineer for five years when she was promoted to team lead. She was thrilled about the opportunity but also felt a sense of unease. She had never managed people before and wasn't sure if she had what it took to be an effective leader.

In her first few weeks as team lead, Abigail struggled. She found herself micromanaging her team, constantly checking in on their progress and dictating how tasks should be done. She also had trouble communicating her expectations clearly, leaving her team members feeling confused and frustrated.

One day, Abigail had a particularly challenging interaction with a team member. They had missed a deadline, and Abigail reacted by publicly reprimanding them in front of the entire team. The team member became defensive, and the situation escalated into a heated argument.

After the incident, Abigail realized she needed to reassess her approach to leadership. She started by reflecting on her own strengths and weaknesses. She recognized that her technical skills had gotten her promoted, but she lacked some of the interpersonal skills needed to lead effectively.

Abigail decided to seek out resources to help her develop her leadership skills. She read books on management, attended workshops, and sought advice from mentors. Through this process, she began to understand the importance of building trust, communicating effectively, and empowering her team members.

One of the key insights Abigail gained was the importance of having a growth mindset. She realized that her fixed mindset had been holding her back. She had been afraid of failure and resistant to feedback, but she now saw these as opportunities for learning and growth.

Abigail also worked on developing her emotional intelligence. She practiced active listening, paying attention to her team members' needs and concerns. She learned to manage her own emotions better, staying calm under pressure and avoiding reactive behavior.

As Abigail applied these new skills and mindset, she saw a noticeable difference in her team's performance. Team members were more engaged and proactive, taking ownership of their work. Communication improved, with fewer misunderstandings and conflicts. Abigail also felt more confident in her ability to lead and make decisions.

One of Abigail's proudest moments came when she successfully navigated a project crisis. Instead of micromanaging, she trusted her team to problem-solve and kept communication channels open. The team pulled together and delivered the project on time, with Abigail's leadership presence keeping everyone focused and motivated.

Looking back on her journey, Abigail realizes that becoming an effective leader didn't happen overnight. It required self-awareness, a willingness to learn, and the courage to step outside her comfort zone. But the payoff was worth it. Abigail not only grew as a leader, but she also helped her team reach their full potential and drive better results for the organization.

Abigail's story illustrates that leadership is a skill that can be developed over time. By focusing on the key elements of a leadership mindset, building confidence, and cultivating leadership presence, anyone can become a more effective leader. It starts with understanding your role, recognizing your impact, and committing to continuous growth and improvement.

TWO

Skill #1—Effective Leadership Communication

> *The difference between mere management and leadership is communication.*
>
> Winston Churchill

These words cut straight to the heart of what separates great leaders from average ones. As a leader, your ability to communicate effectively is not just a nice-to-have skill; it's a fundamental requirement for success.

In this chapter, we're going to dive deep into the world of leadership communication. We'll explore why effective communication is so critical, the impact it can have on your team and organization, and the key skills and strategies you need to master to become a great communicator.

But before we get into the nitty-gritty, let's be clear about the goal here: This isn't just about learning some new tips and tricks to add to your leadership toolbox; it's about fundamentally transforming the way you interact with your team and the results you're able to achieve together.

When you communicate effectively, you don't just transmit information; you inspire, motivate, and empower your team to do their best work. You create a sense of shared purpose and direction and build the trust and relationships essential for success.

But here's the thing: Effective communication doesn't come naturally to most people. It's a skill that requires ongoing practice and development. In today's fast-paced, digitally-driven workplace, the challenges of communication are greater than ever before.

That's why this chapter is so important. By the end of it, you'll have a deep understanding of what effective leadership communication looks like, and you'll have a set of practical tools and strategies you can start using right away to improve your own communication skills.

You'll learn how to communicate with clarity and empathy, how to adapt your style to different audiences and situations, and how to use communication to build stronger relationships and drive better results. You'll also learn how to navigate common communication challenges, such as managing conflicts, delivering difficult feedback, and communicating effectively in a remote or digital environment.

The Essentials of Workplace Communication

Communication is the foundation of any organization. It's how we share information, generate ideas, solve problems, and build relationships. As a leader, your ability to communicate effectively can have a huge impact on your team's success. In this section, we'll explore why communication is such a critical skill for leaders and the impact it can have on a workplace.

Why Communication Is an Important Skill for Leaders

Let's be real. Trying to lead a team without being able to clearly convey your expectations, give feedback, or inspire and motivate others is like trying to drive a car without a steering wheel. It's just not going to work. Effective communication is essential for leaders because it allows them to set clear goals and expectations.

You need to be able to articulate the vision and objectives for your team in a way that everyone can understand and get behind. This means clearly communicating what needs to be done, why it's important, and how success will be measured.

Communication is also key to building strong relationships with your team members. When you communicate openly, honestly, and frequently, you're more likely to earn their trust and respect. This can lead to higher levels of engagement, productivity, and retention. As a leader, you're also responsible for helping your team members grow and develop. This means providing regular feedback, both positive and constructive, and coaching individuals to help them improve their skills and performance. Effective communication is essential for delivering feedback in a way that is clear, specific, and actionable.

Finally, you need to be able to communicate effectively to resolve conflicts and challenges. Conflicts and challenges are a part of any workplace. As a leader, you need to be able to identify issues, understand different perspectives, and find solutions that work for everyone involved. This requires active listening, empathy, and the ability to facilitate productive conversations.

The Impacts of Strong Workplace Communication

When communication is strong within a workplace, the benefits are huge. One of the most important impacts is boosted morale and engagement. When team members feel heard, valued, and informed, they're more likely to be engaged and motivated in their work. Strong communication helps create a positive work environment where people feel connected to each other and the larger goals of the organization.

Effective communication also enables team members to work together more seamlessly. When everyone is on the same page and has a clear understanding of their roles and responsibilities, it's easier to collaborate and achieve common goals. This improved cooperation and collaboration can lead to increased productivity and efficiency. Clear communication helps to reduce misunderstandings, errors, and delays. When team members have the information they need to do their jobs well, they can work more efficiently and productively.

Strong communication also facilitates the exchange of ideas and perspectives, which can lead to better problem-solving and decision-making. When team members feel comfortable sharing their thoughts and opinions, it can lead to more creative and effective solutions.

Communication Skills for a Workplace

So, what does it take to be an effective communicator in the workplace? One of the most important skills is active listening. Being a good listener is just as important as being a good speaker. Active listening means giving your full attention to the person speaking, asking clarifying questions, and reflecting back what you've heard to ensure understanding.

Effective communicators are also able to convey their message clearly and concisely. In a busy workplace, it's important to be able to organize your thoughts, use plain language, and get to the point quickly. Adapting to your audience is another key skill. Different people have different communication styles and preferences. Effective communicators are able to adapt their message and delivery to their audience, whether it's a one-on-one conversation or a presentation to a large group.

Nonverbal communication is also important. Your body language, tone of voice, and facial expressions all contribute to how your message is received. Effective communicators are aware of their non-verbal cues and use them to reinforce their message and build rapport.

Giving and receiving feedback is another critical communication skill in the workplace. Effective communicators are able to deliver feedback in a way that is specific, actionable, and supportive, while also being open to receiving feedback themselves.

Finally, empathy and emotional intelligence are essential for effective communication. Being able to understand and respond to the emotions of others is a critical skill. Leaders with high emotional intelligence are able to build stronger relationships, resolve conflicts more effectively, and create a more positive work environment.

By developing these communication skills, leaders can create a workplace culture that values open, honest, and productive communication. This can lead to higher levels of trust, collaboration, and ultimately, success for the team and the organization as a whole.

Managing Communication: The Basics

As a leader, how you communicate can make or break your team's success. It's not just about what you say but how you say it. In this section, we'll explore some practical tactics and strategies for communicating effectively with your team.

Psychological Communication Tactics for Leaders

First, let's talk about some psychological communication tactics that can help you encourage positivity and communication without seeming unapproachable or mean.

- **Use "I" statements.** Instead of saying, "You always mess up," try, "I feel frustrated when deadlines are missed." This shifts the focus from blame to your own feelings and experiences, making the conversation less confrontational.
- **Ask open-ended questions.** Instead of asking, "Did you finish the report?" try, "How's the report coming along?" Open-ended questions encourage dialogue and show that you're interested in their perspective.
- **Practice active listening.** When someone is speaking, give them your full attention. Avoid interrupting, and reflect back what you've heard to ensure understanding. This shows that you value their input and helps build trust.
- **Give specific, actionable feedback.** Instead of saying, "Good job," try, "I really appreciated how you handled that client meeting. Your preparation and attention to detail really made a difference." Specific feedback helps people understand what they're doing well and where they can improve.
- **Use positive reinforcement.** When someone does something well, acknowledge it. This could be as simple as

a thank you or a public recognition. Positive reinforcement encourages people to continue doing good work and helps create a positive team culture.

- **Be mindful of your tone.** The way you say something can be just as important as what you say. Avoid sarcasm or a condescending tone and aim for a neutral or positive tone instead.
- **Lead by example.** If you want your team to communicate openly and respectfully, you need to model that behavior yourself. Be open, honest, and respectful in your own communications, and others will follow suit.

Empathetic Communication Strategies for Leaders

Empathy is a key skill for leaders. When you can put yourself in someone else's shoes and understand their perspective, you can communicate more effectively and build stronger relationships. Here are some techniques for communicating with empathy:

- **Validate their feelings.** If someone comes to you with a problem or concern, start by acknowledging their feelings. Say something like, "I can understand why you're feeling frustrated," or "That must have been really challenging for you." This shows that you've heard them and that their feelings are valid.
- **Ask questions to understand.** Don't assume you know the full story. Ask questions to gain a deeper understanding of their perspective. "Can you tell me more about what happened?" or "How did that make you feel?" These questions show that you're interested in their experience and want to understand.
- **Show that you're listening.** Use nonverbal cues like nodding, maintaining eye contact, and leaning in to show

that you're engaged in the conversation. Paraphrase what they've said to ensure you've understood correctly.

- **Offer support.** Once you understand their perspective, offer your support. This could be in the form of resources, advice, or simply a listening ear. Show that you're there to help them in whatever way you can.
- **Follow up.** After the conversation, follow up to see how they're doing. This shows that you care about their well-being and that the conversation wasn't just a one-time event.

Fostering Interpersonal Communication in the Workplace

As a leader, it's not just about your own communication skills. You also have a responsibility to foster effective communication among your team members. Here are some ways you can encourage interpersonal communication in the workplace:

- **Create opportunities for casual interaction.** Encourage your team members to take breaks together, eat lunch together, or participate in team-building activities. These casual interactions help build relationships and foster a sense of camaraderie.
- **Establish clear communication channels.** Make sure your team knows how to communicate with each other. This could be through email, instant messaging, project management tools, or regular team meetings. Clear communication channels ensure that everyone knows how to get in touch and that no one is left out of the loop.
- **Encourage open and honest feedback.** Create a culture where feedback is welcomed and encouraged. This means modeling the behavior yourself by regularly asking for

feedback and being open to constructive criticism. Encourage your team to do the same with each other.

- **Provide communication training.** Not everyone is a natural communicator. Provide training and resources to help your team develop their communication skills. This could be in the form of workshops, online courses, or mentorship programs.
- **Celebrate successes together.** When your team achieves a goal or milestone, celebrate together. This could be as simple as a team lunch or a public recognition. Celebrating successes together helps build a sense of team spirit and reinforces the importance of working together.

Remember, communication is a skill that takes practice. As a leader, it's your job to set the tone and create an environment where open, honest, and respectful communication is the norm. By using these tactics and strategies, you can build a team that communicates effectively and works together seamlessly.

Digital Mayhem: Communication in the Digital Workplace

In today's world, the workplace is no longer confined to a physical office. With the rise of remote work and digital communication tools, the way we communicate with our teams has changed dramatically. While these tools have many benefits, they also come with their own set of challenges. As a leader, it's important to know how to effectively communicate with your team in a digital environment.

One of the biggest challenges of digital communication is the lack of nonverbal cues. When we communicate face-to-face, we rely heavily on things like facial expressions, tone of voice, and body language to convey meaning and build rapport. In a digital environment, these cues are often missing, which can lead to misunderstandings and miscommunications. In order to mitigate this, it's important to be as clear and concise as possible in your digital communications. Use simple language, avoid jargon or acronyms that may not be familiar to everyone, and be specific about what you need or expect.

Another challenge of digital communication is the potential for information overload. With so many different communication channels available, it's easy for messages to get lost or overlooked. In order to combat this, clear guidelines should be established as to which communication channels should be used for which purposes. For example, you might use email for more formal communications, instant messaging for quick questions or updates, and video conferencing for more in-depth discussions or team meetings. It's also important to be mindful of the frequency and timing of your communications. Don't bombard your team with constant messages or expect immediate responses at all hours of the day.

When it comes to managing remote teams, it's important to make an extra effort to foster a sense of connection and collaboration. One way to do this is to schedule regular check-ins or team meetings via videoconferencing. This allows everyone to see each other's faces and feel more connected, even if they're not in the same physical location. It's also a good idea to create opportunities for casual interaction and team-building, such as virtual coffee breaks or happy hours.

Finally, as a leader, it's important to model good digital communication habits for your team. This means being responsive and available but also setting clear boundaries around your own time and availability. It means being respectful and professional in all your digital communications, even if the tone is more casual than it might be in person. It means being open to feedback and willing to adapt your communication style as needed to meet the needs of your team.

Communicating effectively in a digital workplace requires a different set of skills and strategies than traditional face-to-face communication. By being clear and concise, establishing guidelines for communication channels, fostering a sense of connection and collaboration, and modeling good communication habits, you can help your team navigate the challenges of digital communication and thrive in a remote work environment.

Wrapping Up

In this chapter, we've explored the critical role of communication in leadership and the workplace. We've discussed why effective communication is essential for leaders, the impact it can have on a team and organization, and the key skills needed to communicate successfully.

We've covered key concepts, including:

- the importance of clear, empathetic, and adaptable communication for leaders
- the benefits of strong workplace communication, such as increased engagement, collaboration, and productivity
- psychological tactics and empathetic strategies for communicating effectively with team members
- common communication challenges in the workplace and how to manage conflicts and difficult conversations
- strategies for communicating effectively in a digital workplace and fostering connection and collaboration in remote teams

By mastering the art of effective communication, you can build stronger relationships, foster a more positive and productive work environment, and achieve better results as a leader. Remember, communication is a skill that requires ongoing practice and development. By continually working to improve your communication skills, you can become a more confident, capable, and inspiring leader.

However, effective communication is just one piece of the leadership puzzle. In the next chapter, we'll explore another critical skill for leaders: developing and communicating a clear vision and strategy. You'll learn how to set a compelling direction for your team, align everyone around a common purpose, and drive results through strategic thinking and planning.

So, if you're ready to take your leadership to the next level and inspire your team to achieve great things, keep reading. The best is yet to come.

Case Study: Brian

Brian had always been a strong individual contributor. His technical skills were top-notch, and he consistently delivered high-quality work. So, when he was promoted to a leadership role, he assumed that his skills would naturally translate. However, he quickly realized that leading a team required a whole new set of communication skills.

At first, Brian struggled. He was used to working independently and didn't know how to effectively communicate his expectations or provide feedback to his team. He often found himself getting frustrated when team members didn't meet his standards, but he didn't know how to express this constructively.

One day, after a particularly challenging team meeting, Brian reached out to his mentor, Natalie. Natalie had been in leadership roles for over a decade and was known for her exceptional communication skills.

In their meeting, Natalie asked Brian to describe some of the communication challenges he was facing. As Brian shared his struggles, Natalie listened intently and asked clarifying questions. She then shared a few key insights that struck a chord with Brian.

First, Natalie emphasized the importance of clarity in communication. She advised Brian to be specific and clear when setting expectations and providing feedback. "Don't assume that your team can read your mind," she said. "Be explicit about what you need and why it matters."

Next, Natalie talked about the power of empathy in communication. She encouraged Brian to put himself in his team members' shoes and try to understand their perspectives. "When you communicate with empathy, you build trust and rapport," she explained. "Your team will be more open to your feedback and more motivated to meet your expectations."

Finally, Natalie stressed the importance of adaptability in communication. She advised Brian to tailor his communication style to the needs and preferences of each team member. "Some people prefer direct, to-the-point communication, while others appreciate more context and explanation," she said. "The key is to be flexible and adjust your approach as needed."

Armed with these insights, Brian started to make some changes. He began each project by clearly outlining his expectations and the desired outcomes. He made a point to check in with each team member regularly, not just to monitor progress but to understand their challenges and provide support.

When providing feedback, Brian focused on being specific and constructive. Instead of just pointing out what wasn't working, he offered suggestions for improvement and acknowledged progress along the way. He also made an effort to really listen to his team members and understand their perspectives.

Over time, Brian started to see a noticeable difference in his team's performance and morale. Team members were more engaged and proactive, and there were fewer misunderstandings and conflicts. Brian himself felt more confident and effective in his leadership role.

One of the most rewarding moments came during a project post-mortem. A team member shared how much they appreciated Brian's clear communication and supportive leadership throughout the project. They noted how Brian's approachability and willingness to listen made them feel valued and motivated to do their best work.

For Brian, this feedback was a testament to the power of effective communication. He realized that by focusing on clarity, empathy, and adaptability, he could not only improve his own leadership skills but also bring out the best in his team.

Brian's journey illustrates that effective communication is a skill that can be learned and developed over time. By being intentional about how we communicate and continually seeking to improve, we can become better leaders and drive better results for our teams and organizations.

THREE

Skill #2—Priorities and Strategic Thinking

Do not follow where the path may lead. Go instead where there is no path and leave a trail.

Ralph Waldo Emerson

A s a leader, one of your most important responsibilities is to set the direction for your team and organization. But in today's fast-paced and ever-changing business environment, it can be challenging to know where to focus your efforts and how to align your team around a common purpose.

That's where the skills of prioritization and strategic thinking come in. By learning how to set clear priorities, create a compelling vision, and make decisions that drive results, you can become a more effective and impactful leader.

In this chapter, we'll explore the art and science of prioritization and strategic thinking. You'll learn how to identify the most important goals and initiatives for your organization and how to communicate them in a way that inspires and motivates your team.

We'll discuss the role of vision in leadership and how to craft a clear and compelling vision that guides your team's efforts and decision-making. You'll learn strategies for effective prioritization, such as using data, engaging your team, and being ruthless about saying no to distractions.

We'll also examine the value of strategic thinking and how it can help you anticipate challenges, identify opportunities, and make informed decisions. You'll learn methods for fostering strategic thinking in yourself and your team, such as conducting SWOT analyses, scenario planning, and embracing experimentation.

Finally, we'll discuss how to motivate and empower your employees to prioritize and strategize on their own. You'll learn techniques for communicating the "why" behind your priorities, providing autonomy and support, and modeling strategic thinking in your own leadership practice.

By the end of this chapter, you'll have a toolkit of skills and strategies for setting priorities, creating a vision, and thinking strategically. You'll be better equipped to lead your team and organization with clarity, purpose, and impact.

So let's dive in and explore the power of prioritization and strategic thinking. With these skills in your arsenal, you'll be ready to blaze your own trail and lead your team to new heights of success and achievement.

How Leaders Impact Workplace Prioritization

As a leader, one of your most important roles is helping your team prioritize their work. It's not just about assigning tasks and setting deadlines—it's about providing clarity and direction so everyone knows what matters most.

When you take the time to clearly communicate priorities, you give your team a roadmap for success. They know where to focus their energy and how their individual work fits into the bigger picture. Without that guidance, people can easily get overwhelmed or bogged down in tasks that don't really move the needle.

But prioritization isn't just about efficiency—it's also about empowerment. When you involve your team in the prioritization process and give them the context they need to make informed decisions, you show that you trust and value their judgment. That kind of ownership and autonomy can be incredibly motivating.

The Value of Prioritization

Let's be real—we've all had those days where we feel like we're drowning in to-do lists and email notifications. That's why prioritization is so crucial in the workplace.

When we take the time to step back and identify what's truly important, we can cut through the noise and focus on the work that has the greatest impact. We're able to use our time and energy more effectively, which leads to better results and less stress.

Prioritization also helps us adapt to change. In today's fast-paced business environment, priorities can shift quickly. If we're not clear on what matters most, we risk getting sidetracked by shiny objects or falling behind when new challenges arise.

How Vision Informs Priorities

So how do we determine what our priorities should be? That's where vision comes in. As a leader, your job is to paint a picture of the future you want to create and rally your team around that shared purpose.

A clear vision gives everyone a North Star to guide their decisions and actions. It helps us stay focused on the big picture and avoid getting bogged down in the day-to-day grind. When we know where we're headed, it's easier to prioritize the work that will get us there.

But crafting a compelling vision takes work. It has to be aspirational enough to inspire but also grounded enough to feel achievable. It has to be communicated clearly and consistently so everyone understands their role in bringing it to life.

Some key elements of a strong vision include:

- a sense of purpose that goes beyond just making money
- a clear picture of what success looks like
- alignment with the organization's values and culture
- emotional resonance that sparks passion and commitment

Once you have a vision in place, the next step is to break it down into actionable priorities. That might involve setting specific goals and metrics, identifying key initiatives, or mapping out a timeline for implementation.

The important thing is to make sure everyone understands how their work contributes to the larger vision. When people see the purpose behind their priorities, they're more likely to stay motivated and engaged.

Prioritization Strategies for Leaders

Okay, so we know why prioritization matters and how vision guides the process. But what does it actually look like in practice? Here are a few strategies leaders can use to prioritize effectively:

- **Use data to inform decisions.** Look at metrics like customer feedback, sales numbers, or employee engagement scores to identify areas of opportunity or concern.
- **Engage your team in the process.** Ask for input on what they see as the most important priorities and involve them in brainstorming solutions.
- **Be ruthless about saying no.** Not every idea or request is going to be a top priority. Be willing to make tough calls and communicate the reasoning behind them.
- **Regularly reassess and adjust.** Priorities can change over time, so build in opportunities to step back and reevaluate what's working and what's not.
- **Celebrate progress along the way.** Prioritization is hard work—make sure to acknowledge and appreciate the effort your team is putting in to stay focused and aligned.

At the end of the day, prioritization is about making choices. As leaders, it's our job to make sure those choices are guided by a clear vision and a deep understanding of what truly matters to our organizations and our people.

Why Strategizing Matters

As leaders, it's easy to get caught up in the day-to-day grind of putting out fires and managing immediate needs. But if we want to truly move our organizations forward, we have to make time for strategic thinking.

When we step back and look at the big picture, we can identify opportunities for growth, anticipate challenges before they become crises, and make more informed decisions about where to allocate resources. We're able to be proactive instead of just reactive.

Strategizing also helps us align our teams around a common purpose. When everyone understands the larger goals we're working toward and how their individual roles contribute to those goals, they're more likely to feel invested and engaged in their work.

But let's be clear—strategic thinking isn't just about creating a fancy plan that sits on a shelf collecting dust. It's about developing a living, breathing framework that guides our actions and decisions every day. It's about being intentional and adaptable in the face of change.

Common Strategic Methods for Leaders

So, how can leaders foster strategic thinking in themselves and their teams? Here are a few methods to try:

- **Start with the end in mind.** Before diving into tactics and action plans, take time to clarify your ultimate goals and objectives. What does success look like, and how will you know when you've achieved it?
- **Conduct a SWOT analysis.** Take an honest look at your organization's strengths, weaknesses, opportunities, and threats. This can help you identify areas where you need to focus your efforts and resources.

- **Engage in scenario planning.** Consider different possible futures and how your organization might need to adapt in each case. This can help you build resilience and agility in the face of uncertainty.
- **Encourage diverse perspectives.** Bring people with different backgrounds and expertise into the strategizing process. Their unique insights can help you see problems and opportunities in new ways.
- **Embrace experimentation.** Don't be afraid to try new things and learn from failure. The most effective strategies often emerge through a process of iterative testing and refinement.

Motivating Employees to Prioritize and Strategize

Of course, strategic thinking can't just happen at the top levels of an organization. To truly be effective, it needs to be embedded in the culture and practiced by everyone.

As leaders, we can motivate our employees to prioritize and strategize by:

- **Communicating the "why" behind our strategies.** Help people understand how their work fits into the larger picture and why it matters.
- **Giving people autonomy and ownership.** Empower employees to make decisions and take calculated risks in service of our strategic goals.
- **Providing the necessary resources and support.** Make sure people have the tools, training, and guidance they need to be successful.

- **Celebrating progress and learning.** Recognize and reward employees for their contributions to our strategic efforts, even when things don't go as planned.
- **Modeling strategic thinking ourselves.** We can't expect our teams to prioritize and strategize if we're not doing it ourselves. Lead by example and make strategic thinking a visible part of your own leadership practice.

Ultimately, strategic thinking is a muscle that needs to be exercised regularly. It requires discipline, curiosity, and a willingness to challenge assumptions and try new things.

But when we make it a priority as leaders and create a culture that values strategic thinking at all levels, we set ourselves up for long-term success. We become more agile, more innovative, and more resilient in the face of whatever challenges come our way.

So, let's commit to carving out the time and space for strategic thinking in our organizations. Let's ask the hard questions, have the tough conversations, and be willing to take calculated risks in pursuit of our goals.

It won't always be easy, but it will always be worth it. Because when we lead with strategy, we create a brighter future for ourselves, our teams, and the people we serve.

Digital Vision and Priority Setting

Managing remote teams comes with its own set of challenges, especially when it comes to helping employees prioritize their work. When people are working from home, it's easy for the lines between work and personal life to blur, leading to distractions and competing demands on their time and attention.

As leaders, we have to be proactive in supporting our remote employees and giving them the tools and guidance they need to stay focused and productive. That starts with clear communication and expectation setting.

Make sure your team understands what the top priorities are and how their individual work fits into the larger goals of the organization. Have regular check-ins to discuss progress, provide feedback, and adjust the course as needed.

It's also important to recognize that working from home can be isolating and stressful, especially during times of uncertainty. Show empathy and compassion for the challenges your employees may be facing, and be willing to offer flexibility and support where needed.

Encourage your team to set boundaries and create routines that help them manage their time effectively. That might mean blocking off dedicated work hours, taking regular breaks, or finding ways to minimize distractions in their home environment.

Finally, make sure your remote employees have the resources and technology they need to do their jobs effectively. That includes things like reliable internet access, necessary software and tools, and clear processes for collaboration and communication.

Methods for Conveying Managerial Vision Online

Conveying your vision and priorities to a remote team can be challenging, especially when you don't have the benefit of in-person interactions and nonverbal cues. But with the right approach, it's possible to keep your team aligned and engaged even when you're not in the same physical space.

One key is to overcommunicate. When you're not seeing your team face-to-face every day, it's easy for messages to get lost or misinterpreted. Make sure you're regularly sharing updates, reiterating priorities, and providing context for decisions and changes.

Use a variety of communication channels to reach your team, including email, video conferencing, instant messaging, and project management tools. But be thoughtful about which channels you use for different types of messages. For example, sensitive or complex topics may be better suited for a video call than an email.

When you're communicating your vision and priorities, be clear and specific. Use concrete examples and metrics to illustrate what success looks like and break down larger goals into smaller, actionable steps.

Encourage two-way communication and feedback from your team. Create opportunities for them to ask questions, share ideas, and express concerns. This not only helps ensure everyone is on the same page but also fosters a sense of ownership and engagement in the work.

Finally, don't underestimate the power of storytelling. Share examples of how your team's work is making a difference and contributing to the larger vision. Celebrate successes and milestones, and recognize the effort and dedication of your employees.

Managing remote teams requires a different set of skills and strategies than managing in-person teams. But with intentional communication, clear prioritization, and a focus on empathy and support, it's possible to keep your team aligned and motivated no matter where they're located.

The key is to lead with transparency, consistency, and a genuine commitment to your team's well-being and success. When you do that, you create a culture of trust and accountability that can thrive in any environment.

Wrapping Up

In this chapter, we've explored the critical role of prioritization and strategic thinking in effective leadership. We've discussed how leaders can set clear priorities, create a compelling vision, and motivate their teams to stay focused and aligned, even in the face of change and uncertainty.

We've covered key concepts including:

- the importance of prioritization in managing workloads, focusing on high-impact tasks, and adapting to changing circumstances
- the role of vision in setting a clear direction, aligning teams around a common purpose, and guiding decision-making
- strategies for effective prioritization, such as using data, engaging teams, being ruthless about saying no, and regularly reassessing
- the value of strategic thinking in identifying opportunities, anticipating challenges, and making informed decisions
- methods for fostering strategic thinking, such as starting with the end in mind, conducting SWOT analysis, scenario planning, and embracing experimentation
- techniques for motivating employees to prioritize and strategize, including communicating the "why," providing autonomy and support, and modeling strategic thinking as a leader

By mastering the skills of prioritization and strategic thinking, you can become a more proactive, intentional, and adaptable leader. You can create a culture of purpose and engagement that drives meaningful results and supports the long-term success of your organization.

However, prioritization and strategizing are just one piece of the leadership puzzle. In the next chapter, we'll explore another critical aspect of leadership: decision-making. You'll learn how to make tough choices, navigate complex challenges, and empower your teams to take ownership and initiative in their work.

So, if you're ready to sharpen your strategic thinking skills and lead with greater clarity and impact, keep reading.

Case Study: Marissa

Marissa had been promoted to lead a cross-functional team at her company, tasked with launching a new product line. The project was complex, with many moving parts and stakeholders involved. Marissa knew that to be successful, she would need to prioritize effectively and think strategically.

She started by bringing her team together to create a shared vision for the project. They imagined what success would look like a year from now and worked backward to identify the key milestones and deliverables that would get them there. Marissa made sure everyone understood how their individual work contributed to the larger goals.

Next, Marissa worked with her team to prioritize their efforts. They used data from market research and customer feedback to identify the features and benefits that would have the greatest impact on the product's success. They were ruthless about saying no to ideas that didn't align with their strategic priorities, even when it meant disappointing some stakeholders.

Throughout the project, Marissa encouraged her team to think strategically. They conducted regular SWOT analyses to identify potential risks and opportunities and engaged in scenario planning to prepare for different possible outcomes. When they encountered challenges or setbacks, they used experimentation and iteration to find new solutions.

Marissa also made sure to motivate and support her team along the way. She communicated the "why" behind their priorities and decisions and gave team members autonomy to make choices and take ownership of their work. She celebrated their progress and learning, even when things didn't go as planned.

In the end, Marissa's team successfully launched the new product line on time and on budget. The product was well-received by customers and exceeded initial sales projections. Marissa's leadership and strategic thinking skills have been critical to their success.

Reflecting on the experience, Marissa realized that prioritization and strategic thinking were muscles that needed to be exercised regularly. She committed to making them a core part of her leadership practice going forward and empowering her team to do the same.

FOUR

Skill #3—Decisions and Adaptations for Leaders

Great leaders are not defined by the absence of weakness, but rather by the presence of clear strengths.

John Peter Zenger

As a leader, you are faced with countless decisions every day. Some are small and routine, while others have the potential to shape the future of your team and organization. In a fast-paced and ever-changing business landscape, the ability to make smart, timely choices and adapt to new circumstances is a critical skill for any leader.

But what does it take to be a truly effective decision-maker and flexible leader? It's not just about having access to the right information or being able to think on your feet. Great decision-making and adaptability require specific skills, mindsets, and strategies that enable you to navigate complex challenges with clarity, confidence, and resilience.

In this chapter, you will uncover the secrets to making sound decisions and leading with agility in the workplace. You'll learn why decision-making is crucial for driving results, fostering innovation, and building trust with your team. You'll also gain practical strategies for bouncing back from mistakes and empowering your team to make great decisions.

However, effective leadership is about more than just making good decisions in the moment. It's also about cultivating the flexibility and resilience to adapt to new challenges and opportunities as they arise. In a world where change is constant and disruption is the norm, leaders who can pivot quickly and lead their teams through transitions are the ones who thrive.

That's why this chapter also dives deep into the art of adaptable leadership. You'll explore the key qualities and behaviors of leaders who can navigate uncertainty with ease and learn proven techniques for developing your own flexibility and agility. You'll discover how to lead your team through major changes and transitions and how to foster a culture of innovation and continuous improvement.

By the end of this chapter, you'll have all the skills and strategies you need to become a master decision-maker and an adaptable, resilient leader. Whether you're facing a sudden crisis or a long-term challenge, you'll have the tools to make the right calls, rally your team, and drive results. So, let's dive in and unlock the secrets of great decision-making and leadership agility.

Why Workplace Decision-Making Matters

Decision-making is a fundamental part of both leadership and individual contributor roles in any organization. The ability to make good decisions is critical for driving results, fostering innovation, and adapting to change.

For managers, decision-making is a core responsibility. As a leader, you're often faced with complex challenges and competing priorities. Your decisions can have far-reaching impacts on your team, your customers, and your bottom line. Making the right calls requires a combination of analytical thinking, emotional intelligence, and sound judgment.

But decision-making isn't just important for leaders. Every employee, regardless of their role or level, makes decisions that affect their work and their team's success. When individuals are empowered to make good decisions, they're more engaged, motivated, and productive. They're able to take ownership of their work, solve problems proactively, and contribute to a culture of innovation and continuous improvement.

On the flip side, poor decision-making can have serious consequences. It can lead to missed opportunities, wasted resources, and damage to relationships and reputation. In fast-paced and high-stakes environments, the ability to make smart decisions quickly is essential for staying competitive and achieving goals.

Making Good Decisions as a Leader

So, how can managers make smart workplace decisions? Here's a step-by-step guide:

1. **Define the problem or opportunity.** Clearly articulate what you're trying to solve or achieve. Gather relevant data and information to help you understand the situation.
2. **Identify potential options.** Brainstorm a range of possible solutions or approaches. Consider different perspectives and seek input from others.
3. **Evaluate the options.** Assess the pros and cons of each option. Consider factors such as feasibility, impact, cost, and alignment with organizational goals and values.
4. **Make a decision.** Based on your evaluation, choose the option that you believe will be most effective. Be prepared to explain your reasoning and justify your choice.
5. **Communicate and implement.** Share your decision with relevant stakeholders and outline the next steps to take to put it into action. Establish clear roles, responsibilities, and timelines.
6. **Monitor and adjust.** Track the results of your decision and be open to feedback and course correction as needed. Celebrate successes and learn from failures.

Bouncing Back From Mistakes

Of course, even the best leaders make mistakes sometimes. The key is how you handle them. When you make a decision that doesn't pan out, it's important to:

1. **Own it.** Take responsibility for your mistakes and avoid blaming others or making excuses.

2. **Apologize if necessary.** If your decision had negative impacts on others, acknowledge that and express regret.

3. **Learn from it.** Reflect on what went wrong and what you could have done differently. Identify lessons learned that you can apply to future decisions.

4. **Move forward.** Don't dwell on the mistake or let it paralyze you. Focus on what you can do to recover and make better decisions going forward.

5. **Communicate openly.** Be transparent with your team about what happened and what you're doing to address it. Emphasize learning and growth over perfection.

Encouraging Smart Decisions From Employees

As a manager, you're not the only one making decisions. Your employees are making choices every day that impact their work and your team's results. To encourage smart decision-making at all levels:

1. **Set clear expectations.** Communicate the goals, values, and parameters that should guide decision-making. Make sure everyone understands what success looks like.

2. **Provide training and resources.** Give your team the knowledge, skills, and tools they need to make informed decisions. Offer opportunities for learning and development.

3. **Empower and trust.** Give employees the autonomy to make decisions within their scope of responsibility. Show that you trust their judgment and have confidence in their abilities.

4. **Foster a culture of experimentation.** Encourage calculated risk-taking and learning from failure. Celebrate successes and share lessons learned from mistakes.

5. **Model good decision-making.** Lead by example and demonstrate the kind of decision-making you want to see from your team. Be transparent about your own thought process and decision criteria.

Ultimately, decision-making is both an art and a science. It requires a combination of analytical thinking, intuition, and emotional intelligence. As a leader, your job is to make the best decisions you can with the information available and to create an environment where everyone is empowered to do the same.

Focusing on decision-making as a key leadership skill means you can drive better results, foster innovation, and build a culture of ownership and accountability. When mistakes happen, you can use them as opportunities for growth and learning rather than letting them define you or hold you back.

Cognitive Biases in Decision-Making

As a leader, being aware of the cognitive biases that can cloud your judgment is crucial for making sound decisions. Two common biases that can trip up even the most experienced decision-makers are:

Confirmation bias: the tendency to seek out and favor information that confirms your existing beliefs while discounting evidence that contradicts them. For example, if you're convinced that a certain strategy is the best way forward, you may unconsciously gravitate toward data points and opinions that validate that view and gloss over warning signs.

Overconfidence bias: the inclination to overestimate your abilities, knowledge, and accuracy of predictions. Overconfidence can lead you to take excessive risks, ignore dissenting perspectives, and fail to plan for worst-case scenarios.

To guard against these and other cognitive biases:

- **Actively seek out disconfirming evidence.** Make a habit of asking, "What information would change my mind about this decision?" and "What data might I be missing that would paint a fuller picture?" Encourage your team to play devil's advocate and surface potential risks and downsides.
- **Calibrate your confidence.** Regularly test your knowledge and predictions against objective benchmarks. Keep a decision journal to compare your forecasts to actual results over time. Aim to develop an accurate sense of what you know, what you don't know, and what's inherently uncertain.
- **Invite diverse perspectives.** Assemble a team with varied backgrounds and viewpoints to pressure-test your assumptions and raise alternative approaches. Consult subject matter experts and frontline employees to round out your understanding of complex issues.
- **Use structured decision-making tools.** Frameworks like SWOT analysis, decision trees, and premortems can help you methodically map out options, probabilities, and contingencies. By externalizing your thinking, you can spot flaws and gaps more easily.
- **Beware of high emotions.** Stress, anxiety, and fatigue can exacerbate cognitive biases and impair decision-making. When stakes are high, deliberately slow down, reexamine your underlying mental models, and reconnect with your purpose.

Remember, even the best-laid plans can go awry due to unforeseen factors. Stay humble in your convictions and be ready to pivot as situations evolve. By combining rigorous analysis with openness to changing course, you can nimbly navigate shifting conditions while avoiding preventable mistakes.

The Importance of Adaptability

In today's rapidly changing business environment, adaptability is a critical skill for successful leadership. When you're able to pivot quickly in response to new challenges and opportunities, you're better equipped to drive results and maintain a competitive edge.

Adaptable leaders are able to navigate uncertainty and ambiguity with confidence. They're open to new ideas and approaches, and they're willing to take calculated risks to achieve their goals. They're also able to inspire and motivate their teams to embrace change and adapt alongside them.

But adaptability isn't just about reacting to external circumstances. It's also about proactively seeking out opportunities for growth and improvement. Adaptable leaders are constantly learning and evolving, and they encourage their teams to do the same.

Flexibility Hacks for Leaders

So, how can you develop your own adaptability and flexibility as a leader? Here are some practical tips:

1. **Embrace a growth mindset.** View challenges as opportunities for learning and development rather than as threats or obstacles.

2. **Practice active listening.** Seek out diverse perspectives and be open to feedback and new ideas from your team and stakeholders.

3. **Experiment and iterate.** Don't be afraid to try new approaches and make adjustments based on what you learn. Embrace a culture of continuous improvement.

4. **Communicate openly and transparently.** Share information and insights with your team, and be honest about what you know and don't know in times of change.

5. **Prioritize self-care.** Take care of your own physical, mental, and emotional well-being so that you have the resilience and energy to adapt to new challenges.

Handling Sudden Workplace Changes

Sometimes, change comes suddenly and unexpectedly. Whether it's a crisis, a shift in market conditions, or a new directive from leadership, the ability to adapt quickly is essential.

When faced with sudden change, it's important to:

1. **Stay calm and focused.** Take a step back to assess the situation objectively, and avoid getting caught up in the emotional responses of others.

2. **Communicate clearly and frequently.** Keep your team informed about what's happening and what it means for them. Be transparent about what you know and don't know, and provide regular updates as the situation evolves.

3. **Prioritize and focus.** Identify the most critical priorities and focus your team's efforts on addressing them. Be willing to let go of less important tasks or projects if necessary.

4. **Engage your team.** Involve your team in problem-solving and decision-making, and empower them to take ownership of their work in the face of change.
5. **Lead by example.** Model the kind of adaptability and resilience you want to see from your team. Demonstrate a positive attitude and a willingness to embrace change.

Encouraging Employee Flexibility

As a leader, you're not the only one who needs to be adaptable. Your team members also need to be able to pivot and adjust to new circumstances. To encourage flexibility in your employees:

1. **Communicate expectations clearly.** Make sure your team understands the goals and priorities and how they may need to adapt their work to achieve them.
2. **Provide support and resources.** Give your team the tools, training, and support they need to be successful in the face of change.
3. **Empower decision-making.** Give employees the autonomy to make decisions and take ownership of their work within clear guidelines and parameters.
4. **Celebrate and reward adaptability.** Recognize and appreciate team members who demonstrate flexibility and resilience in the face of change.
5. **Foster a culture of learning.** Encourage ongoing learning and development and create opportunities for employees to acquire new skills and knowledge.

Honing a Resilient Workplace

Ultimately, adaptability and flexibility are about building resilience—the ability to bounce back from setbacks and challenges and continue moving forward.

To create a resilient workplace, focus on:

1. **Building strong relationships.** Foster a sense of connection and trust among team members and encourage open communication and collaboration.
2. **Promoting well-being.** Prioritize the physical, mental, and emotional health of your team, and provide resources and support to help them manage stress and build resilience.
3. **Encouraging innovation.** Create a culture that values creativity, experimentation, and continuous improvement, and empower employees to take calculated risks and learn from failures.
4. **Celebrating successes.** Take time to acknowledge and celebrate achievements and milestones, even in the face of change and uncertainty.

As a leader, your ability to adapt and be flexible is essential for driving results and building a resilient team. By embracing change, empowering your employees, and fostering a culture of learning and innovation, you can navigate even the most challenging circumstances with confidence and success.

Helping Remote and Hybrid Workers Adapt

The COVID-19 pandemic has accelerated the trend toward remote and hybrid work, and it's clear that this new way of working is here to stay. As a leader, it's your responsibility to help your team adapt to this new reality and thrive in a digital workspace.

One of the biggest challenges of remote work is maintaining a sense of connection and engagement among team members. When people are working from different locations and time zones, it's easy for communication and collaboration to break down.

To help your team adapt to a remote or hybrid setting, focus on:

1. **Establishing clear expectations and guidelines.** Make sure everyone understands their roles, responsibilities, and deliverables and how they're expected to communicate and collaborate with one another.
2. **Providing the right tools and technology.** Invest in the software, hardware, and infrastructure your team needs to work effectively from anywhere and provide training and support to help them use these tools effectively.
3. **Fostering a sense of community and belonging.** Create opportunities for social interaction and team building, even if it's virtual. Encourage people to share personal updates and stories and celebrate milestones and achievements together.
4. **Prioritizing well-being and work–life balance.** Recognize that remote work can be isolating and stressful, and encourage your team to take breaks, set boundaries, and prioritize self-care. Model these behaviors yourself, and be open about your own struggles and challenges.

5. **Encouraging open communication and feedback.** Create channels for regular check-ins and feedback, both one-on-one and as a team. Be proactive about seeking input and addressing concerns, and be transparent about your own thoughts and decisions.

6. **Providing flexibility and autonomy.** Trust your team to manage their own time and workload, and give them the freedom to work in ways that are most effective for them. Focus on outcomes and results rather than micromanaging their day-to-day activities.

7. **Offering opportunities for learning and development.** Invest in your team's skills and knowledge, and provide resources and support for ongoing learning and growth. Encourage people to take on new challenges and stretch themselves, even in a remote setting.

Adapting to a remote or hybrid workplace is an ongoing process, and it requires patience, flexibility, and a willingness to experiment and learn. As a leader, your role is to create an environment where your team can thrive, regardless of where they're working from.

By focusing on communication, collaboration, well-being, and growth, you can help your team navigate this new normal with confidence and success. And by embracing the opportunities and challenges of remote work, you can build a more resilient, adaptable, and innovative organization for the future.

Wrapping Up

In this chapter, we've delved into the vital role of decision-making and adaptability in effective leadership. We've explored why the ability to make smart, timely choices and pivot skillfully in the face of change is indispensable for driving results and building resilient teams.

We've covered key concepts including:

- the impact of a leader's decision-making process on team trust, motivation, and performance
- the importance of seeking out diverse perspectives, weighing tradeoffs objectively, and communicating decisions transparently
- cognitive biases like confirmation bias and overconfidence that can derail decision-making, and how to guard against them
- the necessity of adaptability and course correction in an uncertain and rapidly changing business landscape
- strategies for making sound decisions quickly while also staying open to pivots based on new information
- the value of framing mistakes and changes as learning opportunities to build a culture of psychological safety and continuous improvement

By strengthening your skills in effective decision-making and adaptable leadership, you can position yourself and your team to navigate complexity, seize opportunities, and thrive in even the toughest of circumstances. Remember, honing your judgment and agility is an ongoing process that requires humility, curiosity, and a commitment to growth. By continually working to refine these abilities, you can become the kind of leader that people trust to steer them through uncharted waters.

But making great decisions and adapting to change are only part of what it takes to lead a high-performing team. Equally important is the ability to deeply motivate and inspire your people to bring their best selves to their work. In the next chapter, we'll unpack the art of motivating and inspiring others as a leader.

You'll discover techniques for tapping into people's intrinsic drive, cultivating a sense of purpose and meaning, and sparking discretionary effort. We'll explore how to create the conditions for people to do their most creative and impactful work, and how to help them build resilience in the face of setbacks. We'll also study real-world examples of leaders who have ignited genuine inspiration in their teams, fueling remarkable achievements.

If you're excited to learn how to engage the hearts and minds of your people and take your collective performance to new heights, Chapter 5 awaits.

Case Study: Michael

A midsize enterprise software company was riding high in early 2020. They had just closed a record-breaking quarter and were gearing up for a major product launch. But when the COVID-19 pandemic hit, everything changed overnight.

CEO Michael Johnson watched in disbelief as the economy ground to a halt and businesses slashed IT budgets. The company's sales pipeline evaporated, and the product launch suddenly looked like a huge risk. Michael knew he had to act fast to save the company, but the path forward was anything but clear.

Gathering his leadership team on a somber video call, Michael laid out the challenge ahead. "We're in uncharted waters," he said. "But we have a choice. We can either let this crisis paralyze us, or we can face it head-on and find a way to adapt. I believe we have the resilience and creativity to not only survive this but come out stronger."

Michael's first priority was to get a clear picture of the company's financial runway and risk exposure. He pored over cash flow projections and burn rate analyses with the CFO, stress-testing various scenarios. Based on a sober assessment of the data, Michael made the difficult decision to freeze hiring, cut non-essential spending, and furlough 15% of staff. He communicated the news to the company with transparency and empathy, pledging to support impacted employees and restore jobs as soon as conditions improved.

Next, Michael turned his attention to reevaluating the company's product strategy. With businesses cutting costs, the original plan to introduce a premium-priced upgrade now seemed tone-deaf. Michael assembled a team to rapidly prototype a pared-down version of the software that could be offered at a discount to cash-strapped clients. They tested the concept with a group of loyal customers and iterated based on feedback. In parallel, Michael directed the sales team to proactively reach out to every client to offer flexibility on payment terms and explore how the company could support their changing needs.

These decisive moves bought the company breathing room, but Michael knew they weren't enough to secure its future. He needed to find a way to drive new revenue in a recessionary environment. Studying industry data and talking to peers, Michael spotted an intriguing opportunity. With remote work surging, many companies were struggling to manage software spending across a newly-distributed workforce. The company's core product helped IT departments optimize software licensing—could it be adapted to solve this pain point?

Michael green-lit a project to rapidly develop and test a new product line around remote software asset management. The initiative was a departure from the company's roadmap, but

Michael reasoned that extraordinary times called for extraordinary moves. He gave the team wide latitude to experiment, fail fast, and course-correct as they dialed in product-market fit and a go-to-market plan.

Incredibly, within two months, the team had a viable prototype that was getting rave reviews from beta users. Michael made the bold decision to acquire a small startup with complementary technology to accelerate development. He reallocated resources and budgets from other areas to support a full-scale launch, convinced that the market opportunity justified the risk.

The bet paid off. The new product line took off, more than compensating for softness in the company's core business. Energized by the success, Michael began looking for other ways to help clients navigate the challenges of remote work. He launched a thought leadership series on the future of software management and convened a customer advisory board to shape the company's product vision. Internally, he instituted a program to upskill furloughed workers and welcomed them back as the business stabilized.

By the end of 2020, the software company was not only back on solid footing but charting an ambitious new course. Annual recurring revenue was up 15%, employee engagement had never been higher, and the company was celebrated as a shining example of innovative leadership in a crisis.

Looking back, Michael credited the company's resilience to a combination of data-driven decision-making, creative problem-solving, and a willingness to boldly adapt. "In a crisis, you have to confront reality, but you can't let it dictate your options," he reflected. "Our success came from grounding ourselves in facts but having the courage to imagine and pursue a new future. It wasn't a straight line, but by staying nimble and involving our whole team, we found our way forward."

This software company's story illustrates the power of decisive, adaptable leadership in the face of disruption. By balancing clear-eyed realism with bold innovation and aligning his team around shared priorities, Michael was able to steer the company through its darkest hour and unlock incredible new opportunities. The experience left the organization more resilient, united, and growth-oriented than ever—a testament to the art of effective crisis leadership.

Add Your Thoughts to the Conversation on Great Leadership

"Great leaders are not defined by the absence of weakness, but rather by the presence of clear strengths."

John Peter Zenger

When you take on a leadership role, the sudden realization that you have to demonstrate a host of new skills you never needed before—such as psychological communication, setting priorities for your teams, and enhanced resilience—may seem daunting. You were promoted because you are good at what you do. You are a thought leader, with knowledge to share and a work ethic that marks you among the best. Yet in your previous post, you may not have been required to utilize as many people skills—and as a manager, the way you run your team directly impacts their motivation, productivity, and commitment to your organization in the long term.

In your new role, between your hard and soft skills, the latter may be more relevant than ever before. What's more, the need for digital innovation and the rise of remote work require you to rely on new tools, strategies, and technologies to keep your team members focused, goal-oriented, and united.

Being a manager pushes you to be your best, most comprehensive, and flexible self. It requires you to be the spark that creates diverse, forward-thinking, positive teams that embrace change instead of shying away from it. Yet it is possible to rise to all these challenges, so long as you have the information, commitment, and willingness to experiment, practice, and adapt as needed.

My aim throughout this book has been to show readers that excelling at leadership is not a mystery; it involves embracing specific strategies and techniques that, when used alongside a growth mindset, can help you be your own best teacher. If these tips have put you on course to be the kind of leader you always admired in your early days in business, then I hope you can let others know what they will find here.

By leaving a short review on Amazon, you can let other managers know that every day is a new opportunity to discover and utilize the skills they need to help their teams achieve even the most ambitious goals.

Thank you for your support. Thought leaders enjoy sharing the knowledge they gain. I hope you sign up for this cause and lead other readers to the information they are seeking.

Scan the QR code below:

FIVE

Skill #4—Motivating and Inspiring

If your actions inspire others to dream more, learn more, do more, and become more, you are a leader.

John Quincy Adams

As a manager, one of your most important roles is to motivate and inspire your team to do their best work. When employees feel motivated and engaged, they are more creative, productive, and committed to the organization's success. But what does it take to be a truly motivational leader? How can you tap into people's intrinsic drive and ignite a sense of passion and purpose?

In this chapter, we'll explore the art and science of motivational leadership. You'll learn why motivation matters so much in today's workplace and gain practical strategies for energizing your team and bringing out the best in each individual. We'll also discuss how to sustain your motivation and resilience as a leader and adapt your approach to remote and hybrid teams.

By the end of this chapter, you'll have a toolkit of proven techniques for engaging hearts and minds and inspiring extraordinary performance. Whether you're leading a small project team or a large department, you'll be equipped to create an environment where motivation flourishes and amazing things happen.

Your Role as a Leader: How Leaders Motivate and Inspire

At its core, leadership is about mobilizing people to achieve shared goals and bring a vision to life. And motivation is the fuel that propels people forward, even in the face of challenges and uncertainty. As a leader, you have a unique opportunity and responsibility to awaken motivation in your team.

Research shows that there are several key things that the most motivational leaders do:

- **Paint a compelling vision.** They vividly describe where the team is headed and why it matters, creating an exciting, meaningful goal to rally around. They connect day-to-day work to the bigger picture.
- **Believe in their people.** They see the potential in each person and communicate high expectations and confidence that their people can achieve great things. They share ownership and decision-making.
- **Tailor their approach.** They take time to understand what uniquely drives each individual and flex their leadership style to bring out the best in different people. They look for opportunities to align tasks with talents and interests.
- **Lead by example.** They model the energy, optimism, work ethic, and values they wish to see in others. Their passion and commitment is contagious. They're willing to roll up their sleeves and pitch in.

- **Celebrate successes.** They shine a spotlight on wins and accomplishments, giving credit and praise generously. They turn setbacks into learning opportunities. They keep the team's eyes on the horizon.
- **Invest in relationships.** They prioritize one-on-one time to get to know their people as human beings. They show genuine caring and concern. They're quick to offer support and slow to judge.
- **Communicate openly.** They share information transparently, explaining the "why" behind decisions. They solicit input and feedback. They listen as much as they talk.
- **Develop their people.** They provide stretch opportunities, guidance, and resources to help team members build skills and advance. They position themselves as coaches, not bosses.

By consistently applying these practices, you can dramatically increase the motivation and engagement of your team. You create an environment of trust, ownership, growth and recognition that meets people's deep psychological needs and unleashes discretionary effort (Hagberg, 2020).

How to Keep Yourself Motivated as a Leader

Of course, to motivate others, you first need to motivate yourself. Leading people is deeply rewarding but can also be draining, especially in times of change and challenge. To sustain your own drive and resilience:

- **Reconnect with your purpose.** Reflect regularly on your "why"—the unique impact you want to have as a leader. What legacy do you want to leave? What difference do you hope to make for your team, your customers, and the world?

- **Invest in self-care.** You can't pour from an empty cup. Prioritize rest, exercise, hobbies, and time with loved ones. Build the habit of mini-renewals throughout the day—a walk around the block, a chat with a friend, a few minutes of deep breathing.
- **Surround yourself with support.** Cultivate a diverse network of peers, mentors, and coaches who believe in you and challenge you to be your best. Lean on them for brainstorming, advice, and encouragement. Join a mastermind group or find an accountability partner.
- **Keep learning.** Continuously upgrade your leadership skills through books, podcasts, workshops, and stretch projects. Stay curious and look for new ideas to experiment with. Learning stimulates and energizes us.
- **Embrace the tough stuff.** Remember that breakdowns often precede breakthroughs. When the going gets tough, reframe obstacles as opportunities to grow. Focus on what you can control and let go of the rest. Celebrate small wins and signs of progress.

Leading others is a marathon, not a sprint. By deliberately cultivating your own motivation and resilience, you position yourself to energize others over the long haul. Don't forget to cut yourself slack and savor the journey. Your team will feed off your engagement.

Motivating a Team: Why a Motivated Team is a Good Team

Now, let's talk about why team motivation matters so much and what it looks like in action. Quite simply, motivation is the secret sauce of standout teams. When a team is fired up, they:

- **Tackle challenges with gusto.** They see obstacles as exciting puzzles to solve rather than threats to avoid. They go the extra mile to get results.
- **Generate game-changing ideas.** They embrace fresh thinking and healthy debate. They build on each other's ideas to innovate beyond the status quo.
- **Collaborate seamlessly.** They share information openly, ask for help readily, and put the team agenda first. There's a palpable sense of loyalty and pride.
- **Rebound from setbacks quickly.** They treat failures as learning opportunities. They bounce forward with grit and optimism.
- **Proactively improve processes.** They don't settle for the way things have always been done. They relentlessly look for ways to streamline, simplify, and automate.
- **Provide outstanding service.** They go out of their way to delight internal and external customers. They communicate with empathy and build lasting relationships.
- **Attract and retain top talent.** They rave about their team to others. People are lining up to join and no one wants to leave.

Simply put, motivated teams run circles around disengaged ones. With the pace of change accelerating and the war for talent heating up, organizations can't afford the productivity tax of lackluster motivation. It's your job as a leader to unleash the latent potential and enthusiasm of your people.

Strategies for Motivating a Team

So, how do you motivate a team day in and day out? Here are some tried and true plays to add to your repertoire:

- **Set clear goals and expectations.** Make sure the team understands exactly what success looks like and how their efforts contribute. Clarify roles and decision rights. Align on norms for communication, meetings, conflict, etc.
- **Provide meaningful work.** As much as possible, design jobs and projects to tap into individuals' strengths, values, and interests. Help people see the impact of their work on stakeholders.
- **Grant autonomy.** Give people the freedom to figure out how to achieve agreed-upon objectives in their own way. Provide guardrails and support, but resist micromanaging.
- **Check in regularly.** Schedule frequent one-on-ones just to see how team members are doing. Ask what they're enjoying, what they're struggling with, and how you can help. Show you care about them as humans first.
- **Invest in relationships.** Create opportunities for the team to get to know each other as people—coffees, lunches, volunteer projects, and so on. Relationships grease the wheels of collaboration.
- **Be a coach.** Ask questions more than you give answers. Offer feedback that is timely, specific, and actionable. Have career conversations about individuals' aspirations, strengths, and growth areas.
- **Recognize good work.** Celebrate milestones, wins, and effort along the way, not just end results. Use a variety of rewards—public/private, financial/non-financial, individual/team. Be timely and sincere.

- **Keep it fun.** Insert play, humor, and friendly competition when you can. Laughter is a powerful antidote to stress. Start a meeting with a silly icebreaker or organize a team trivia night.
- **Mix it up.** Variety wards off boredom and stagnation. Rotate people into new roles, invite guest speakers, and hold meetings in new venues. Introduce a "wild card" item to spark creative thinking.

The key is to see motivation as an ongoing practice, not a one-time event. Different people are motivated by different things, and even the same person's needs change over time. Keep experimenting, observing, and adapting. Motivation is an art as much as a science.

Encouraging Collaboration

An especially powerful way to boost team motivation is to foster a collaborative culture. When team members freely share ideas, resources, and support, they challenge each other to reach new heights. Here are some ways to encourage collaboration on your team:

- **Build psychological safety.** Create an environment where people feel safe to speak up, experiment, and admit mistakes without fear of retribution. Model vulnerability and inclusive behaviors.
- **Break down silos.** Expose the team to stakeholders and experts in other parts of the organization. Encourage them to build relationships and learn about other functions' needs or pressures.
- **Use collaboration tools.** Provide technology that makes it easy for the team to brainstorm, share files, provide input,

and coordinate work—tools like Slack, Microsoft Teams, Trello, Asana, Mural, and so on.

- **Assign group projects.** Look for opportunities for team members to partner on tasks and initiatives. Mix up combinations to strengthen team-wide relationships.
- **Provide constructive conflict training.** Help the team learn to disagree productively by focusing on issues, not personalities, asking questions to understand, and seeking win-win solutions. Intervene when debates get personal.
- **Set shared goals.** Create some objectives and metrics that the whole team is jointly responsible for delivering. Consider linking part of the team's compensation to collective results.
- **Showcase collaboration successes.** Publicly highlight examples of collaboration that produced great outcomes for customers, the business, and the team. Tell stories that reinforce "we" over "me."

When collaboration is the norm, team members feel like they're part of something greater than themselves. They stretch and achieve more together than they ever could alone. And that's motivating!

Positive Reinforcement Strategies

Finally, one of the simplest yet most powerful ways to motivate is to reinforce the behaviors you want to see more of. When you consistently acknowledge and reward people's efforts and successes, they're more likely to repeat those behaviors in the future. Try these positive reinforcement strategies:

- **Be specific.** Rather than just saying, "Good job," describe exactly what you observed and appreciated. "I noticed how you went out of your way to incorporate feedback from the client. That attention to detail will really strengthen the relationship."

- **Reward improvement, not just results.** Motivation fizzles if the bar for recognition seems out of reach. Look for opportunities to praise progress, milestones, and growth along the way to big goals. "I know you've been working hard to get more comfortable with public speaking. Leading that presentation today was a real breakthrough—you seemed much more at ease."

- **Tailor recognition to individuals.** One size definitely does not fit all when it comes to rewards. Get to know what kinds of acknowledgments are most meaningful to each person. One team member might crave public praise, while another prefers a thoughtful email or small gift.

- **Encourage peer-to-peer recognition.** Positive reinforcement shouldn't just come from leaders. Set up easy ways for team members to celebrate each other— kudos boards, shout-outs in team meetings, spot bonuses they can give. Amplify the appreciation.

- **Make it a habit.** Weave appreciation into the fabric of how the team operates. Try ending each day by reflecting on a "win" large or small. Or start one-on-ones by sharing one thing you value about the person.

Remember, what gets recognized gets repeated. Make positive reinforcement your secret weapon for motivation. As the old saying goes, "People may forget what you said, but they'll never forget how you made them feel."

The Powers of Team Building

Speaking of helping a team feel valued and connected, one of the most underrated tools in a leader's motivation toolbox is team building. Team building is all about giving people a chance to get to know each other as humans and form authentic relationships. When done well, it's like rocket fuel for collaboration, creativity, and fun.

What Is Team Building?

At its core, team building is any activity that brings a team together to socialize, problem-solve, and play outside of day-to-day work. Classic examples include volunteer projects, escape rooms, improv workshops, cooking competitions, scavenger hunts, and outdoor adventures.

The key is to design activities that create shared memories, surface unique talents, and invite people to let their guard down. The most powerful team-building moments often have nothing to do with the work itself.

Why Team Building Is Important

If team building sounds like just a "nice to have," think again. Investing in team building can yield concrete results like:

- stronger communication and collaboration, as people feel more comfortable sharing ideas and asking for help
- increased motivation and engagement, as people feel more connected to their teammates and the larger purpose
- improved problem-solving, as people learn to leverage each other's diverse experiences and think outside the box

- greater innovation, as psychological safety and creative abrasion fuel risk-taking
- higher productivity, as people are energized to go the extra mile for each other
- better talent retention, as strong workplace relationships are a powerful antidote to burnout

In today's world of remote and hybrid work, team building is more important than ever for combating isolation and building culture. And it doesn't have to be expensive or time-consuming to be effective. Try these easy DIY team-building exercises:

Team Building Exercises

Exercise #1:

Scavenger hunts are a fun way to encourage people to work together in a different context. Try a "getting to know you" variation:

Split the group into pairs or trios and give them a list of personal tidbits to learn about each other, like: favorite book/movie/food/vacation, hidden talent, bucket list, walk-up song, and so on.

Have them snap a photo of their team when they finish and share a few highlights with the larger group.

Debrief by reflecting on commonalities, surprises, and new appreciations.

Exercise #2:

A little bit of healthy competition is a great way to get people laughing and putting their heads together. Try an improv game with a teamwork twist:

Ask for a volunteer to leave the room. Then, give the group a random scene to act out without using any words—for example, preparing a holiday meal or cleaning up after a natural disaster.

Invite the volunteer back in and have them try to guess the scene based on the group's motions and facial expressions.

Rotate through several volunteers. Vote on a winning scene based on creativity, clarity, and teamwork.

Debrief by highlighting great examples of people paying attention to each other, building on each other's ideas, and making each other look good—all hallmarks of strong ensemble work!

Exercise #3:

Taking the team offsite for a day or even an overnight retreat can work wonders for helping them gel and recharge. To get the most bang for your buck:

Choose a location that feels special and at least a little bit indulgent—a cool hotel, a scenic park, or a funky space. A change of scenery signals a break from the daily grind.

Build in a mix of structured discussions or activities focused on the team's purpose, progress, and challenges, *as well as* freeform social time like meals and games. Aim for a 60/40 split.

Capture key insights, decisions and commitments and follow up on them after the retreat. An offsite shouldn't just be a fun time-out; it should move the team forward.

The options for team building are endless. The main thing is to approach it thoughtfully, with clear goals and an experimental mindset. Poll the team on what kinds of activities interest them. Enlist volunteers to help plan. Gather feedback and keep iterating. The team that plays together stays together!

Cooperating, Sharing Ideas, and Listening to the Needs of WFH Employees

These days, with so many teams working remotely or in hybrid arrangements, leaders need to be especially intentional about motivating from a distance. It's all too easy for WFH teammates to feel isolated, disconnected, and disengaged. Here are some ways to keep your remote employees motivated and create a strong virtual team culture:

- **Check in frequently one-on-one.** With impromptu hallway chats off the table, it's important to proactively schedule regular video check-ins with each direct report. Prioritize rapport and trust-building, not just project updates. Listen more than you talk.
- **Make remote meetings interactive.** Staring at a screenful of faces on mute is a surefire motivation killer. Designate a rotating facilitator to keep people engaged with polls, brainstorms, breakouts, and action plans. Carve out time for informal catch-ups, too.
- **Level the playing field.** Combat "presence bias" by making sure remote participants in hybrid meetings have equal airtime and influence as people in the room. Invest in technology like Meeting Owl that allows everyone to be seen and heard clearly.
- **Create a virtual water cooler.** Start a "random" channel in your team chat app for memes, articles, music playlists, and casual conversation. Hold virtual coffees, happy hours, and lunch and learns.
- **Send care packages.** Every once in a while, surprise and delight your remote team members with a token of appreciation delivered to their homes—a book, a gift card, a yummy treat. It's a tangible way to show you're thinking

of them.

- **Encourage setting boundaries.** Promote a "work from home, not live at work" ethic by inviting folks to share their preferred communication hours, response times, self-care practices, etc. Model healthy habits yourself.
- **Offer remote perks.** Provide benefits tailored to WFH life like home office stipends, flexible schedules, wellness apps, and learning opportunities. Show that you're invested in your remote employees' success and quality of life.
- **Celebrate the whole person.** Make a point of acknowledging people's lives outside of work—new babies, moves, marathons, hobbies, and so on. Start meetings with an optional "proud and personal" minute for folks to share recent highlights.

With intention and creativity, you absolutely can create a vibrant, motivating culture for a remote or hybrid team. The key is to prioritize connection and to keep experimenting with new ways to help your people feel seen, valued, and part of something special, no matter where they're working.

Wrapping Up

In this chapter, we've delved into the vital role of motivation and inspiration in effective leadership. We've explored why the ability to energize and engage people is indispensable for driving performance and creating a thriving team culture.

We've covered key concepts, including:

- the impact of a leader's vision, belief, and example on igniting people's intrinsic motivation

- the importance of tailoring motivation strategies to individuals' unique drivers and needs
- the power of meaningful work, autonomy, recognition, and fun in fueling team performance
- strategies for encouraging collaboration and using team building to forge strong interpersonal bonds
- the necessity of investing in one's own motivation and resilience to sustain leadership over the long haul
- techniques for motivating remote and hybrid teams through intentional communication and virtual culture-building

By strengthening your skills in motivational leadership, you can unleash the full potential of your people and accomplish remarkable things together. Remember, motivating is an ongoing practice that requires compassion, experimentation, and genuine care for your team's growth and well-being.

When you commit to this practice, you'll reap incredible rewards. You'll see your team stretch, innovate, and achieve beyond what they thought possible. You'll tackle even the toughest challenges with courage and solidarity. And you'll leave a lasting impact as a leader who uplifted others and made work a source of meaning and fulfillment.

So keep flexing your motivation muscles, one interaction at a time. Get curious about what makes your people light up, and relentlessly look for opportunities to align their superpowers with the team's mission. Don't be afraid to get creative and have fun along the way!

And on those inevitable days when your own motivation dips, take heart: your team needs your authentic, caring presence more than a flawless facade. Reconnect with your "why," lean on your support system, and extend yourself some grace. Your commitment to your own growth and humanity is a gift to those you lead.

In the next chapter, we'll build on the foundation of motivation to explore another critical leadership skill: empowerment and delegation. You'll learn how to equip your team with the tools, trust, and courage to step up and drive their own success. Get ready to amplify your impact and cultivate the leaders of tomorrow.

Case Study: Samuel

Samuel Upshaw was a rising star at his software company, having just been promoted to lead a critical new product launch. He inherited a team of talented engineers, designers, and marketers, but they seemed demoralized and disengaged after months of pivots and setbacks.

Samuel knew he needed to quickly establish himself as a leader who could rally the troops and reignite their passion for the project. He started by scheduling one-on-one meetings with each team member to understand their motivations, frustrations, and ideas.

In their very first team meeting, Samuel painted a vivid picture of the impact their product could have on customers' lives. "Imagine a world where small businesses can compete with the big guys because our software levels the playing field," he said. "That's the mission we're on together."

Samuel backed up his words with actions. He fought for the resources and support the team needed to do their best work. He rolled up his sleeves and dove into the trenches, troubleshooting alongside his developers.

To rebuild a sense of camaraderie, Samuel organized optional weekly lunches where the team could bond over non-work topics. He started a ritual of kicking off each sprint planning meeting with "shout-outs" where people could celebrate each other's progress and acts of teamwork.

When the pressure was on, Samuel was the team's biggest cheerleader. "I know this release is high-stakes, and the deadlines are tight," he acknowledged. "But I've seen what this team is capable of, and I have total faith that we'll rise to the challenge. Let's show everyone what we're made of!"

Samuel made a point of being transparent about the "why" behind decisions that impacted the team, even when the news was tough. When he had to cut a beloved feature to meet the launch date, he explained the tradeoffs and invited the team to problem-solve alternatives.

To keep the team engaged, Samuel looked for opportunities to tailor assignments to individuals' interests and development goals. He gave the more junior designer a stretch project leading the UX research. He nominated the senior engineer to present at a prestigious conference.

As the launch date approached and the team was clocking long nights and weekends, Samuel pulled out all the stops to keep morale high. He surprised them with their favorite coffee and snacks. He gave spot bonuses to those going above and beyond. He even convinced his boss to give the whole team an extra day off after the launch to recharge.

When launch day arrived, Samuel gathered the team to pop champagne and reflect on how far they'd come. "I couldn't be prouder of what we've accomplished together," he told them, his voice filled with emotion. "Thanks to your creativity, grit, and teamwork, we're poised to change the game for our customers. Savor this moment—you've earned it!"

The team met the launch deadline, and the initial customer feedback was glowing. More importantly, they had gelled into a tight-knit unit that was energized for the next big challenge. As Samuel watched them high-five and hug after the last deliverable was out the door, he knew exactly why he led: to help talented people come together and achieve extraordinary things.

This case study shows the power of motivational leadership in action. By investing in relationships, communicating a compelling vision, removing obstacles, celebrating milestones, tapping into individuals' strengths, and making work meaningful and fun, Samuel transformed a struggling team into a high-performing one. He proved that with the right conditions and encouragement, people will move mountains.

SIX

Skill #5—Empowerment and Delegation-Leadership Tools

Leadership is about empowering others to achieve things they did not think possible.

Simon Sinek

E very manager faces moments when they feel stretched too thin. With mounting workloads, tight deadlines, and a barrage of meetings and emails, it can start to feel like there simply aren't enough hours in the day. However, as leaders, one of the most powerful tools in our toolkit is the ability to empower our teams and delegate tasks effectively. When done right, delegation enhances productivity, develops employee skills, and frees managers to focus on higher-level strategic work.

However, many leaders struggle with letting go and trusting others to handle important assignments. We convince ourselves it will be faster to just do it ourselves. But ultimately, this management style is unsustainable and will cap your potential as a leader. In this chapter, we'll explore the what, why, and how of empowerment and delegation. You'll gain the confidence and practical techniques to unleash your team's full potential while optimizing your own leadership capacity.

Enhancing Teamwork Through Delegation—What Is Delegation?

At its core, delegation is the act of assigning responsibility for a task to someone else, typically a subordinate employee. Rather than tackling everything ourselves, we entrust capable team members to handle pieces of a project based on their unique skills, experience level, and development goals.

Consider these real-world examples of delegation in action:

- A marketing director delegates social media management to a digital strategist. This person crafts posts, interacts with followers, and tracks analytics, freeing the director up to focus on big-picture brand strategy.
- An IT manager who is tapped to lead a major cybersecurity overhaul delegates components like firewall configuration, penetration testing, and employee training modules to specialized team members.
- A retail store manager delegates opening/closing procedures, restocking, and merchandising to shift leaders. This allows the manager to dedicate time to inventory forecasting, employee coaching, and customer feedback analysis.

In each case, the leader assessed who was best equipped to handle each task and clearly communicated expectations. With delegation, managers are not relinquishing ultimate accountability. Rather, we're empowering employees as partners in executing team goals.

Benefits of Delegation

When leaders become adept at delegation, the benefits ripple across the entire organization. Effective delegation:

- **Expands team capacity and boosts productivity.** With more hands on deck to tackle initiatives, teams can take on ambitious projects and meet deadlines.
- **Builds team capability.** As employees stretch their skills through progressively challenging assignments, they gain the experience and confidence to make greater contributions.
- **Enhances employee engagement.** Having a direct impact on team success is motivating and helps people find greater purpose and fulfillment in their work.
- **Improves talent retention.** Invested employees who feel valued are more likely to stick around for the long haul. Delegation shows that you see team members' potential.
- **Frees up managers to lead.** With trusted employees handling tactical execution, leaders can invest time in strategic planning, cross-functional collaboration, and developing people.

Delegation vs. Irresponsibility

A common reason managers hesitate to delegate is fear of losing control or being perceived as shirking their duties. However, there's a clear distinction between effective delegation and simply offloading tasks to others. Responsible delegation involves:

- matching the right work to the right person based on their skills and goals

- setting clear expectations around desired outcomes, resources, and timelines
- granting appropriate authority to make relevant decisions
- establishing checkpoints and feedback loops to monitor progress
- remaining ultimately accountable for the work product
- sharing credit and recognition upon successful completion

In contrast, irresponsible offloading may look like:

- haphazardly assigning tasks with little thought to individual fit
- providing scant direction, then micromanaging or swooping in at the 11th hour
- expecting employees to achieve outcomes without sufficient resources or support
- failing to track progress or provide timely course-correction
- blaming subordinates rather than owning overarching accountability
- hoarding credit for positive results and downplaying the team's contributions

Responsible delegation requires upfront planning, ongoing communication, and appropriate follow-up. But the results—an empowered, productive team—are well worth the investment.

How to Delegate Tasks

Now that we've covered the delegation fundamentals let's explore how you can delegate effectively starting today.

Play to the Strength of the Team

Exceptional delegation begins with tapping into what each team member does best and enjoys most. Get to know your employees' skills, experience, working styles and aspirations. Use team meetings, one-on-ones and project debriefs to draw out these insights.

Armed with this knowledge, look for opportunities to delegate tasks that align with each person's strengths. The employee who is an Excel wizard can tackle the data analysis, while the one with a flair for design can own the client presentation deck. Be sure to delegate meaty, impactful assignments beyond just the low-level, mundane tasks. Show confidence in your rising leaders by trusting them with work that develops new muscles.

As you delegate, paint a clear picture of what success looks like. Align on concrete goals and milestones, then get out of the way and let the team work its magic with guardrails and support to keep things on track.

Ask, Don't Force

A surefire way to tank an employee's motivation is to simply dump an unsavory assignment on their plate without context or consideration for their skills and bandwidth. Instead, engage team members in a two-way dialogue about the work that needs to be done and how they might be able to contribute.

Share your rationale on why you felt they could excel at the task and how it benefits them and the broader team. But also give space for them to share concerns, ideas, and what support they'll need. When people have a say in structuring their work, they'll be far more invested than if simply handed a to-do list.

Balance Delegation With Responsibility

As a manager, you are ultimately accountable for your team's results, even when delegating execution to others. So, it's critical to set up a cadence of checkpoints and progress reports to ensure work is progressing as planned.

Your level of involvement should flex based on the complexity of the work and the employee's experience level. A seasoned veteran may simply need a quick weekly status report, while a junior employee will benefit from more hands-on coaching and problem-solving along the way.

Upfront, align with employees on your expectations for updates, resource needs, and how you'll course-correct if issues arise. With clear accountability and communication rhythms, you can empower your team while keeping your finger on the pulse of key initiatives.

Workplace Empowerment

While some use the terms interchangeably, there is an important distinction between motivation and empowerment. Motivation is about influencing people's desire to act. Empowerment is about enabling people's ability to act.

Think of it this way: Motivation is the fuel, while empowerment is the vehicle. To truly unleash your team's potential, you need to both inspire their commitment and remove barriers in their way. Here are strategies to ignite empowerment across your organization:

Empowering and Building Up Employees

True empowerment has to start at the top with leaders who deeply value employees' ideas and contributions. Demonstrate empowerment in your everyday interactions by:

- seeking input before making decisions that impact the team
- encouraging people to openly share ideas and constructive feedback
- acknowledging and appreciating excellent work
- investing in learning and development to expand employees' capabilities
- granting people the flexibility to approach their work in fresh, creative ways
- having employees' backs if they make well-intentioned mistakes while taking smart risks
- passing the baton to let rising leaders take the lead on initiatives

Empowering employees also means having candid conversations about the skills and behaviors needed to advance. Work with team members to co-create specific, actionable development plans so expectations are concrete.

Encouraging Independence and Individual Leadership

Employees can't feel truly empowered if their manager is always hovering or swooping in to take over at the first sign of trouble. Set your team up for success, and then step back and let them rise to the occasion.

Align on goals, resources, and checkpoints, then grant employees leeway in how they execute their pieces of work. Serve as a sounding board and safety net, but don't micromanage. This gives people room to tap their unique skills and ideas to achieve outcomes rather than simply following prescriptive steps.

Celebrate moments when team members proactively identify and solve problems before they escalate. Praise employees who speak up with ideas to optimize the work, even if it means respectfully challenging the "way we've always done it."

When you encourage independent thinking and create space for team members to find their leadership sea legs, you build organizational bench strength and free yourself up to focus on the strategic work only you can do.

Empowering Online: How to Empower Your Virtual Employees

With remote and hybrid teams now the norm, it's critical that leaders adapt their empowerment and delegation skills to this virtual world.

Physical distance can make it even more tempting to tightly manage employees' day-to-day execution. Resist this urge. A "butts in seats" mindset will only breed resentment among remote employees.

Instead, align on crystal clear goals, roles, and success measures. Then, give remote workers flexibility to structure their days and tap their preferred working styles to achieve strong outcomes. Focus on concrete outputs rather than micromanaging activity.

It's also important to intentionally create virtual spaces for casual connection and idea-sharing that might happen more organically in an office. Consider hosting virtual coffee chats or designating the first few minutes of Zoom meetings for personal catchups to foster relationships.

Proactively celebrate remote employees' contributions and share positive feedback openly with the broader team. With fewer organic "great job!" moments, virtual workers especially value knowing their impact is seen and appreciated.

Delegating Virtual Tasks

In a remote setting, delegating can feel like chucking work into a virtual black hole. Without clear expectations and rhythms for collaboration, it's easy for wires to get crossed. Set virtual delegation up for success with strategies like:

- Document processes, handoffs, and timelines in a central location like a team wiki or project plan. Don't assume everyone knows how to do the work.
- Translate high-level objectives into bite-sized tasks and milestones. Remote workers will appreciate a clear roadmap to guide their efforts.
- Scheduling regular one-on-one video chats to check in on progress and problem-solve. With fewer organic touchpoints, these planned connections are critical.
- Establish communication norms for the team, such as which channels to use for various topics, expected

response windows, and so on. A shared understanding streamlines virtual collaboration.

- Leverage collaboration tools that boost transparency and coordination. A robust project or task management platform keeps everyone aligned on the next steps.
- Resist the urge to overdo check-ins and status updates. Build trust by giving virtual workers space to execute productively, with guardrails when needed.

With a conscious effort to plan, align, and enable your remote team, virtual delegation and empowerment can yield the same powerful results as in a traditional office.

Wrapping Up

In this chapter, we've explored the transformative power of empowerment and delegation in leadership. We've seen how these skills unlock the full potential of teams, enabling employees to stretch their capabilities, take ownership of their work, and make meaningful contributions to shared goals.

We've covered key concepts, including:

- the definition of delegation and real-world examples of how it enhances team capacity and productivity
- the benefits of effective delegation for employee development, engagement, and talent retention
- the distinction between responsible delegation and irresponsible task dumping
- strategies for delegating successfully by aligning tasks with employees' strengths, engaging in two-way planning, and maintaining appropriate oversight

- the difference between motivation (inspiring action) and empowerment (enabling action) and the importance of both
- techniques for empowering employees through trust, autonomy, development, and visible appreciation
- the necessity of adapting empowerment and delegation approaches for remote and hybrid teams through clear expectations, streamlined processes, and intentional communication

By honing your skills in empowerment and delegation, you can elevate your leadership impact and build a team of confident, capable contributors who drive outsized results. Remember, empowering others is an ongoing journey that requires trust, communication, and a willingness to let go of some control in service of growth.

When you embrace this journey, the rewards are immense. You'll see your team members tackle new challenges with enthusiasm and ingenuity. You'll have more time and headspace to focus on the strategic, big-picture priorities that truly demand your focus. And you'll gain a reputation as a leader who uplifts others and brings out the best in people.

So start small and keep practicing. Look for one opportunity this week to delegate a meaty project to a team member who's ready to step up. Work together to map out a plan, align on checkpoints, and put your full confidence behind them. Then, watch as they rise to the occasion and exceed even their own expectations.

And on those days when letting go feels uncomfortable, remember that your team's growth and fulfillment is the ultimate measure of your leadership success. Stay focused on the end goal of a more empowered, effective organization and trust the process.

In the next chapter, we'll turn our attention to another critical pillar of exceptional leadership: integrity and ethics. You'll learn why leading with strong principles is non-negotiable in today's world and how to navigate the gray areas with wisdom and authenticity. Get ready to strengthen your moral compass and inspire others through the power of your example.

Case Study: Erin

Erin was a talented marketing manager at a fast-growing tech startup. Her team was responsible for a dizzying array of initiatives, including digital ad campaigns, content strategy, PR, events, and more. As the company grew, so did the demands on Erin's team. Late nights and weekend work became the norm as they raced to keep up with the breakneck pace.

Erin found herself overseeing every tactical detail, terrified that a single dropped ball could derail their success. She was up until 2 a.m. obsessively polishing the copy and design of every client email. She sat in on every vendor meeting to ensure talking points were perfectly on-brand. She even insisted on personally approving the menu for the quarterly client appreciation event.

While Erin's team appreciated her dedication and high standards, they also began to feel stifled and disengaged. It seemed Erin didn't fully trust them to handle important work. They hesitated to share new ideas or take risks, knowing Erin would likely rewrite their plans anyway. Talented employees began to leave for companies that offered more runway to make an impact.

One evening, as Erin was about to dive into another round of campaign micromanagement, she had a wake-up call. At this rate, there was no way she or the team could sustain this pace. She knew something fundamental needed to change—and that change had to start with her own leadership approach.

Erin thought back to the training she took on situational leadership and the power of flexing between directing, coaching, supporting, and delegating based on an employee's skill and will for a given task. She realized her default was firmly stuck on "directing" across the board—and it was burning everyone out.

At the next team meeting, Erin vulnerably shared her realization and commitment to lead differently. She acknowledged the toll that excessive oversight was taking on everyone. She shared her confidence in the team's abilities and her excitement to empower them in driving key pieces of work more independently.

Together, they audited their collective workload to determine which initiatives should remain with Erin and which could be owned by other team members. For the first time, Erin dug into each person's unique skills and aspirations to align them with stretch assignments.

Erin worked with each employee to outline clear objectives, milestones, and success measures for their delegated projects. She established a cadence for progress updates and coaching sessions, with the explicit goal of providing support and space to execute their ideas. She practiced biting her tongue and asking curious questions before jumping in with fixes.

As this new rhythm took hold, Erin began to notice a radical transformation across the team. Employees tackled their assignments with renewed energy and pride. Creative ideas flowed freely. Productivity and quality skyrocketed. And perhaps most importantly, people were having fun together again.

With the tactical work in capable hands, Erin was able to focus her attention on higher-value priorities like developing marketing's long-term vision, building cross-functional relationships, and mentoring rising leaders. Her own work became more rewarding and impactful.

While it wasn't an overnight change, through consistent empowerment and delegation, Erin and her team reached new heights together. By letting go and lifting others up, Erin found the secret to sustainable leadership success.

SEVEN

Skill #6—Integrity and Ethical Leadership

> *The supreme quality for leadership is unquestionable integrity.*

Dwight D. Eisenhower

Next up, we have guidelines for acting with integrity and embracing ethical action in leadership. As a leader, your conduct sets the tone for your entire organization. Leading with strong ethics and integrity creates a culture where employees feel valued, motivated and compelled to do their best work. By the end of this chapter, you will have a solid understanding of how to lead with integrity and champion ethical behavior at all levels.

What Is Ethical Leadership?

At its core, ethical leadership means leading in a manner that respects the rights and dignity of others. Ethical leaders consistently strive to be fair, do the right thing, and base their decisions on a strong moral foundation, even when it's not the easiest path.

They communicate openly, consider all stakeholders, accept responsibility for their actions, and hold themselves accountable to a high ethical standard. This commitment to doing what's right —not just what's profitable or expedient—distinguishes the ethical leader.

Ethical leadership involves carefully weighing decisions, being transparent, and ensuring that both the means and the ends are morally sound. It necessitates considering the long-term consequences, not just short-term gains. Ethical leaders foster an environment of trust and integrity, leading by example and inspiring others to uphold similar principles.

They have the courage to make tough calls and stand behind them. At the same time, ethical leaders are not rigid or inflexible. They are open to input, willing to admit mistakes, and adaptable when situations change. Ultimately, ethical leadership is about building organizations and cultures that are not only successful but also principled, humane, and socially responsible. It's a higher standard of leadership but one with enduring value.

Some key traits of ethical leadership include:

- **Integrity:** Being honest, transparent and consistently acting in alignment with one's stated values. An ethical leader walks the talk.
- **Respect:** Treating all people with dignity, compassion, and fairness. Ethical leaders don't play favorites or abuse their power.
- **Service-focused:** Putting the needs of employees, customers, and the greater good above self-interest. The ethical leader serves rather than commands.

- **Concern for justice:** Weighing decisions carefully to avoid unfair practices or harm to others. Ethical leaders ensure people are treated equitably.
- **Value-driven:** Holding oneself and the organization to clearly articulated values and principles. The ethical leader says what they stand for and stands by what they say.

Ethical leadership is especially crucial in turbulent times. When facing challenges or crises, organizations helmed by ethical leaders don't resort to moral shortcuts or desperate measures that could damage their reputation and culture. Instead, their steadfast moral compass allows them to navigate upheaval with their integrity intact.

Benefits of Ethical Leadership

Why does leading with ethics and integrity matter so much? Because it has far-reaching positive impacts on the entire organization.

When leaders consistently model ethical conduct and insist on integrity, it becomes embedded in the company culture. Employees take their cues from the top—if they see leaders cutting corners, they are more likely to relax their own ethical standards. But if leaders walk their talk, it inspires everyone to operate at a higher level.

Some of the key organizational benefits of ethical leadership include:

- **Increased employee engagement and productivity.** When employees feel their leaders are looking out for their interests and committed to doing the right thing, they are more motivated to give their best effort. Research shows employees are more engaged and satisfied working for ethical companies (Ashfaq et al., 2021).

- **Better ability to attract and retain talent.** Workers increasingly want to work for employers whose values align with their own. A company known for ethical, people-first leadership becomes an employer of choice that can win the war for talent. One study found the most ethical companies outperform on key HR metrics like employee loyalty and willingness to recommend the company (Seppälä & Cameron, 2015).
- **Improved business performance.** Organizations led by ethical leaders tend to have stronger core values, less misconduct, and more long-term focus—all of which contribute to better overall performance. The most ethical companies have been shown to outperform their counterparts in terms of stock price and net income.
- **Enhanced brand reputation and customer loyalty.** In today's transparent world, unethical practices quickly come to light and can decimate a company's reputation. Conversely, a strong record of ethical conduct builds brand equity and trust with all stakeholders, leading to more loyal customers.
- **Better risk management.** Ethical leaders foster an environment where employees feel safe speaking up about potential issues before they mushroom into crises. With more openness and accountability, ethical companies are better at proactively spotting and managing risks.

Clearly, integrity and ethics aren't just feel-good concepts—they're good for business. By holding themselves to high ethical standards, leaders create resilient, productive, profitable organizations that stand the test of time.

Signs of Unethical Leadership

Of course, not all leaders live up to these lofty ideals. Power can be intoxicating, and some may let it go to their heads, taking actions that put their integrity into question. Warning signs that a leader may be veering into unethical territory include:

- **Lack of transparency.** Unethical leaders tend to prize secrecy over transparency. They keep decision-making processes opaque, fail to share important information with employees, and discourage open dialogue. This allows unethical practices to stay hidden.
- **Encouraging a "win at all costs" environment.** In a laser focus on the bottom line over all else, unethical leaders may pressure employees to meet unrealistic targets, cut corners or turn a blind eye to wrongdoing. They create an "ends justify the means" culture.
- **Covering up mistakes.** Rather than owning up to missteps and learning from them, unethical leaders may go to great lengths to conceal errors. They play the "blame game" rather than taking responsibility.
- **Failing to address misconduct.** Unethical leaders tend to look the other way when faced with reports of misdeeds. Rather than investigating issues and holding wrongdoers to account, they sweep problems under the rug to protect the organization's reputation.
- **Making decisions in a vacuum.** Unethical leaders may fail to consult or consider the impacts of their choices on employees and other stakeholders. They make unilateral decisions without regard for unintended consequences or concerns raised by others.

- **Disregarding ethics guidelines and compliance procedures.** Even if codes of conduct or ethics hotlines are in place, unethical leaders may treat them as window dressing or impediments to achieving business goals. They bend the rules to suit their agenda.

If you spot these red flags in your organization's leadership, beware. An ethical framework is only as strong as a leader's commitment to consistently upholding it.

Becoming an Ethical Leader

The good news is that becoming an ethical leader is very much within your power. At its heart, ethical leadership is a skill you can actively cultivate—a muscle you can strengthen with practice and commitment.

Some actionable ways to grow your ethical leadership capacity:

1. **Clarify and communicate your values early and often.** Sit down and ask yourself: What do I stand for as a leader? What principles matter most to me? Don't assume employees can read your mind. Make your ethical values explicit by putting them in writing, baking them into company policies, and regularly discussing them one-on-one and in public forums.
2. **Be the first to live by your standards.** As a leader, you need to epitomize the ethical conduct you expect to see. Make sure your own decision-making and behaviors are beyond reproach. Hold yourself to a higher standard than your employees—never fall into a "do as I say, not as I do" mentality.

3. **Hire for ethics and values.** Make integrity a key hiring criterion from the outset. Ask ethics-related questions during interviews, check references carefully, and choose candidates who demonstrate values that align with yours. Building an ethical culture starts with bringing in ethical people.

4. **Provide ethics training.** Don't assume everyone innately knows the right thing to do. Offer thorough training on ethical dilemmas and how to navigate them. Use interactive exercises and case studies to help employees practice thinking through complex situations and upholding company standards.

5. **Reward ethical conduct.** Don't just punish misdeeds—proactively spotlight examples of ethical behavior. Publicly acknowledge employees who make tough choices to do the right thing. Build ethics into your performance reviews and promotion criteria to signal its importance.

6. **Create vehicles for reporting problems.** Cultivate a speak-up culture by providing anonymous hotlines or other safe channels for employees to raise ethical concerns without fear of retaliation. Investigate all complaints thoroughly and take visible corrective action. Proving you'll listen and act helps surface issues early.

7. **Acknowledge the gray areas.** Ethical dilemmas are rarely black and white. Have frank discussions with employees about the nuanced situations they may face. Empower them to trust their judgment and speak up when something feels "off," even if it's not a clear-cut ethical breach.

By weaving ethics into the very fabric of your company in these ways, you cultivate a culture of integrity where everyone is committed to doing the right thing. Remember: Building an ethical culture is an ongoing, never-ending process. Like a garden, it requires constant tending. But the harvest—a company that operates with consistently high moral standards—is worth it.

Encouraging Employee Ethics

As important as your own ethical leadership is, you can't be everywhere at once. For your company to operate with optimal integrity, you need every employee to act as an ethical leader in their own right.

Some ways to encourage ethical conduct from employees:

- **Engage in ongoing ethics dialogues.** Don't just cover ethics once during new hire orientation. Keep the conversation going with regular ethics check-ins, lunch-and-learns, and Q and A sessions. Solicit employee input on ethical dilemmas they're grappling with. The more ethics becomes a two-way, everyday dialogue, the more embedded it becomes in employees' minds.
- **Empower employees to be moral change agents.** Encourage employees to not only follow ethical standards themselves but also to positively influence their peers. Urge them to speak up tactfully when they see others engaging in misconduct. Reframe intervention not as "tattling" but as upholding company values. The more employees feel it's "on them" to shape culture, the more likely they are to take an active role.
- **Make ethics a team sport.** As powerful as your voice as a leader is, peer-to-peer voices are equally important. Consider instituting an ethics advocate program where volunteers from each department serve as ethics resources and champions. Task them with educating

colleagues, surfacing team-specific issues, and brainstorming solutions. This enlists employees as partners in upholding ethics rather than just passive recipients of rules.

- **Incentivize integrity.** Is ethical behavior baked into your employee recognition programs? If not, consider adding an award for the employee who best exemplifies company values each quarter or year. Reward whistleblowers who surface problems and employees who make tough choices to uphold ethics. The more you celebrate moral courage, the more employees will be inspired to choose the high road.
- **Share positive stories.** Don't just talk about ethics in terms of what not to do. Balance cautionary tales with hopeful examples of employees who faced tricky moral situations and navigated them well. Highlight these ethics success stories in newsletters, meetings, and town halls. They provide a road map for how to live your values.

When you get your whole workforce invested in embodying ethics, that's when acting with integrity becomes your company's default mode. And that's a powerful thing.

Integrity in Action

Ethical leadership isn't just a lofty philosophy—it springs from thousands of everyday choices and behaviors. One of the most crucial ways to lead ethically is to consistently act with rock-solid integrity in all you say and do.

At its essence, integrity means being truthful, acting honorably, and treating people fairly. An ethical leader with integrity always strives to:

- **Tell the truth—even when it's hard.** Leaders with integrity don't sugarcoat realities, tell half-truths, or let employees believe false assurances. They communicate openly and candidly, even when the truth is difficult to hear. They know that even small lies or sins of omission can shred leadership credibility.

- **Make decisions based on values, not just financial gain.** Leaders with integrity don't just do what's profitable—they do what's right. They carefully weigh how choices align with company values and benefit all stakeholders. If faced with a decision that would boost the bottom line but violate company ethics, they have the courage to forgo the financial upside in favor of integrity.

- **Deliver on their promises.** Ethical leaders do what they say they're going to do. They don't make commitments that they can't keep or freely discard agreements when they become inconvenient. Following through on promises is the core of who they are.

- **Treat people equitably.** Leaders of integrity don't play favorites or discriminate unfairly. They make a sincere effort to treat all employees with equal respect, regardless of position or personal feelings. Even when they have to make tough calls, they ensure the decision-making process is consistent and above board.

- **Hold themselves accountable.** When an ethical leader makes a mistake, they own it. They don't blame extenuating circumstances or point fingers at others. They acknowledge their responsibility, apologize sincerely, and make things right. This accountability allows them to build real trust.

- **Do the right thing, even under pressure.** Integrity means adhering to your values even when it hurts in the short term. Ethical leaders don't let a stressful situation tempt them into moral shortcuts or unethical actions to save face or limit damage. Their integrity is unshakeable.

Of course, acting with unfailing integrity is often easier said than done. We're all human, and even the most ethical among us may sometimes fall short of our own high standards. What's important is that we keep integrity at the top of our minds, strive to make ethical choices from moment to moment, and quickly correct course when we stray.

We also need to forgive ourselves—and others—when those all too human slip ups happen. An ethical lapse doesn't make someone a bad person or negate an overall track record of integrity. What matters is that sincere remorse is shown, amends are made, and lessons are learned to prevent repeats. An ethical leader acknowledges mistakes, but focuses more on making the next right choice.

The more your words and actions consistently align with your values, the more your integrity shines through. And the more your integrity acts as a beacon, the more employees will trust you and model their behavior on yours. That's why it's so important to sweat the small stuff and get the integrity piece right.

Ethical Leadership in the Virtual World

In today's increasingly virtual environment, practicing ethical leadership and fostering integrity can pose some unique challenges. When teams are dispersed and communicating mainly online, it's all too easy for disconnects to emerge between words typed and real-world actions.

Out of sight can become out of mind when it comes to acting ethically. Someone alone with their computer may feel more tempted to bend the rules or less accountable for moral lapses. Virtual communications often lack the visual cues and personal interactions that reinforce ethics and put a human face on the impacts of one's choices.

Additionally, remote workers grappling with the stresses of an anytime/anywhere workplace may find it harder to resist temptations to cut corners. Employees operating with less direct oversight may feel empowered to play a little fast and loose with standards.

However, the core principles of ethical leadership—open communication, values-driven decision-making, keeping commitments, equitable treatment, accountability, and moral courage—apply whether your team is connecting in person or in pixels. And in some ways, the virtual environment actually makes ethical leadership more important than ever.

With employees feeling isolated and anxious, they need to feel a steady moral keel from leadership. They need to be able to trust that their manager is still making ethical choices and guiding the team with integrity even when they can't see those actions firsthand.

Ethical leadership can be a unifying, grounding force for virtual teams. Anchoring a dispersed workforce in strong, clear values provides a behavioral "north star"—wherever and however people are working. Knowing leadership's commitment to ethics is unwavering fosters a sense of psychological safety and stability during disruption.

Some specific ways to bolster ethics in a virtual setting:

- **Schedule regular face-to-face ethics check-ins.** It's easy to dash off a chat message. It's harder to shade the truth when you have to look someone in the eye. Make time for "face-to-face" ethics conversations with remote employees using video conferencing. Ask them how they're handling stressful situations. Discuss thorny ethical issues as a team to surface misalignments.

- **Highlight integrity role models.** Show that geography isn't a factor when it comes to acting ethically. Give shout-outs to remote employees who demonstrate integrity in a Slack channel. Share examples of virtual team members who upheld ethics in a challenging situation. Making integrity visible shows ethics still apply online.

- **Lean into ethics resources.** When people aren't together physically, they may need extra avenues for raising issues. Make ethics hotlines, chats, or message boards available so remote workers can easily ask questions or report concerns. Check in often to make sure employees know how to access these resources.

- **Reiterate ethics in online communications.** Keep integrity at the forefront of your mind by lacing references to ethics in everyday digital communications. Spotlight a different company value each week in your team e-newsletter. Add ethics questions to your virtual all-hands meeting agenda. The more ethics gets airtime in the online platforms where work happens, the more it stays front and center.

- **Model digital integrity.** Remember, your virtual team is watching how you behave online. If you let venting in the group chat get toxic, shrug off an inappropriate Slack comment, or fail to give credit where it's due in a shared document, that signals the electronic environment plays by different rules. Instead, strive to make your real-world integrity your virtual-world default setting.

Above all, don't let the fact that people aren't together in person become an excuse to relax expectations around integrity. Ethics may take some extra reinforcement in the virtual realm, but they should still be your team's guiding light. Prioritize ethics for remote workers as strongly as you do for those in the office, and integrity will stay intact.

The Road Ahead

As we've seen, ethical leadership and integrity are essential leadership competencies, not nice-to-have qualities. They ensure your company not only survives but thrives long-term. While leading with ethics takes work and isn't always the path of least resistance, the benefits - for your employees, your organization, and yourself —are worth it.

Building your ethical leadership skills is a continuous journey. Pause often to reexamine your values, reflect on your choices, and realign your actions.

As you strive to become an increasingly ethical leader, consider these guiding principles:

- **Make ethics an everyday conversation.** Don't pigeonhole integrity as something you only discuss during annual training. Look for opportunities to engage your team in ongoing dialogues about ethics. Share ethical dilemmas you've navigated as they arise. Ask employees to bring real-world scenarios to the table. The more ethics becomes an open, continuous conversation, the more it will feel second nature.
- **Walk your talk—always.** As a leader, you must assume you're always being watched and judged. Make sure your behaviors consistently reflect your values, even under

stress or when you think no one is looking. Your team will model their actions on how you show up.

- **Strengthen your moral muscle.** Like a muscle, your moral decision-making skills become stronger with use. Each time you make the tough calls to prioritize ethics over expediency, you're training yourself to lead with integrity. Flexing that moral muscle gets easier the more you practice.
- **Surround yourself with ethical voices.** Build a personal "board of directors" filled with people who embody integrity. Seek their input when facing ethical gray areas. They can help you parse difficult situations and stay true to your moral compass. You are the company you keep when it comes to ethics.
- **Stay humble.** Even the most well-intentioned among us will falter sometimes. Resist the urge to label yourself as a paragon of virtue or assume you're above temptation. Acknowledge your human fallibility. That humility will motivate you to stay ever-vigilant and quickly self-correct when you veer off course.
- **Have courage.** Acting with integrity often means taking stands, challenging unethical practices, and making unpopular calls. Muster the moral courage to do what's right, even when it's hard or feels risky. Your ethical leadership will shine brightest in these difficult moments.

As you continue on your ethical leadership journey, know that investing in your integrity is some of the most important work you'll ever do. When you commit to leading ethically and infusing those practices throughout your company, you don't just boost your bottom line—you leave an enduring legacy.

Your actions help shape the leaders of tomorrow. The integrity you model trickles down to influence every employee, who, in turn, carries those ethics forward to shape future organizations. What legacy do you want to leave? A company that creates short-term profit but leaves ethics in tatters? Or an organization known for its unwavering integrity and moral might?

It's up to you. By developing your ethical leadership skills and putting them into practice every day, you set the stage for a rising generation of leaders who insist on integrity. And that's a legacy any leader can be proud of.

Wrapping Up

As we conclude this chapter, take a few moments to reflect on what you've learned. Some key points to reinforce:

- Ethical leadership means consistently leading in a manner that respects the rights and dignity of others. It involves aligning your actions with strong moral principles.
- Ethical leadership benefits your organization across the board—from increased employee engagement and retention to enhanced brand reputation and risk management. Ethics and integrity are essential to your company's long-term success.
- Warning signs of unethical leadership include lack of transparency, covering up mistakes, and disregarding ethics guidelines. Stay alert to any red flags that a leader's integrity is slipping.
- You can cultivate your ethical leadership capacity through steps like clarifying your values, modeling ethical conduct, rewarding integrity, and keeping ethics an open dialogue.

- Encouraging employees to act ethically involves empowering them as moral change agents, making ethics a team sport, and incentivizing integrity.
- Acting with integrity means telling the truth, keeping commitments, treating people equitably, and holding yourself accountable—even when it's difficult. It requires making the right choice in moments big and small.
- Ethical leadership takes on heightened importance in virtual settings, where employees can feel disconnected from company values. Extra reinforcement and digital role modeling of integrity is key.
- Developing your ethical leadership skills is an ongoing journey that requires humility, moral courage, and continuous investment. The enduring positive impact you create is well worth the effort.

As you let these lessons sink in, identify one or two areas where you'd like to focus on strengthening your ethical leadership abilities. Perhaps it's initiating a regular team ethics check-in or being more transparent in your decision-making. Maybe it's recognizing an employee who exemplified integrity or sharing a personal story of an ethical challenge you faced.

Whatever steps you choose, consider them a down payment on the kind of leader you want to be—and the kind of enduring ethical culture you want to create. Know that each choice to prioritize integrity, however small, generates ripple effects that shape the future of your company and the leaders of tomorrow. By developing your ethical leadership skills, you contribute to a rising tide of moral courage that has the power to lift all boats—in your company and beyond.

Now, take a deep breath and step forward with confidence in your ability to lead ethically. Align your actions to your values, insist on integrity, and watch the positive impacts accrue —for your employees, your organization, and yourself. The world is ready for your ethical leadership. It's time to deliver.

Case Study: Amelia

Amelia Hernandez was excited to start her new role as VP of Operations for TechCo, a fast-growing software company. With her decades of experience and track record of success, she felt prepared to help lead the organization to new heights.

However, within her first month, Amelia discovered some concerning practices. Sales reps were routinely overpromising product capabilities to meet aggressive quotas. Quality control checks were being skipped to rush products to market. Senior leaders seemed to turn a blind eye to these issues, as long as targets were hit.

Amelia faced a dilemma. Speaking up could put her reputation and relationships at risk, especially as a new executive. Going along felt like a violation of her values. She knew she had to take action, but smartly.

First, Amelia dug into TechCo's stated values and ethics policies. Integrity and customer focus were touted as core principles—a clear disconnect from what she was seeing. She brought her concerns to the CEO, framing them in terms of these shared values.

"I'm worried that our current practices are eroding customer trust and our reputation," Amelia said. "I'd like to recommend some changes to better align our actions to our values. I believe this will serve us well in the long run, even if it means accepting some short-term tradeoffs."

The CEO was receptive. He acknowledged the issues and invited Amelia to lead an ethics task force to drive solutions across the company.

Amelia started by engaging employees at all levels to surface key ethical risks and brainstorm remedies. She instituted an ethics hotline and an amnesty program for reps to disclose questionable deals without repercussions. She mandated additional product testing and built ethics checks into quality control.

To keep integrity top of mind, Amelia launched monthly ethics training and made values discussions a standing agenda item in leadership meetings. She highlighted employees who made tough calls to uphold ethics and empowered managers to factor integrity into performance reviews. The message was clear: How results were achieved mattered as much as the results themselves.

Amelia knew that real change hinged on her own visible commitment to ethics. She candidly shared her own struggles to balance competing priorities and act with moral courage. She firmly closed deals that couldn't be won without overpromising. Most importantly, she unfailingly modeled the integrity she was asking of others.

Slowly but surely, Amelia saw the culture start to shift. Client satisfaction scores rose, and employee pride grew as TechCo's reputation for "doing it right" spread. Leaders began proactively flagging potential ethical minefields before they exploded. Appeals to ethics held more and more sway in strategic discussions. While it was an ongoing journey, integrity was becoming baked into "the way we do things here."

Amelia's impact extended beyond her tenure. When she eventually moved on to her next challenge, she left behind a leadership team that was passionately committed to ethical conduct, a workforce that felt safe speaking up, and a set of policies and practices that made it easy to act with integrity. TechCo was well on its way to being an enduring ethical powerhouse.

Amelia's story illustrates that while leading ethically isn't always easy, it's always worth it. By insisting on integrity in moments big and small—and inspiring others to do the same—leaders create ripples of positive impact that shape companies and communities for the better. Amelia's ethical leadership didn't just strengthen TechCo in the present—it laid the groundwork for a future in which integrity would remain the company's most precious resource.

EIGHT

Skill #7–Diverse and Inclusive Leadership

When we listen and celebrate what is both common and different, we become a wiser, more inclusive, and better organization.

Pat Wadors

As a leader in today's increasingly diverse and global business landscape, cultivating a culture of inclusivity is no longer optional—it's imperative. Diverse and inclusive workplaces aren't just the right thing to strive for ethically; they drive better business outcomes across the board. Companies that get diversity and inclusion rights are more innovative, more attractive to top talent, and more profitable than their peers. They also happen to be healthier, happier places to work.

But building a truly inclusive organization where diversity is celebrated doesn't happen by accident. It takes committed, intentional leadership to shape a culture where people of all backgrounds feel valued, respected and empowered to succeed. Leaders play a crucial role in setting the tone, modeling inclusive behaviors, and putting equitable practices and policies in place to ensure every employee can thrive.

In this chapter, we'll equip you with the mindset and strategies to become the kind of leader who champions diversity and inclusion, whatever the makeup of your team. By the end, you'll have a deep understanding of why diversity and inclusion matter so much and concrete steps for making them a lived reality. You'll be prepared to leverage the full power of diversity for the benefit of your people and your business. Let's dive in.

Understanding Diversity and Inclusion

First, let's define some key terms. Diversity refers to the full spectrum of human differences, both visible and invisible. It encompasses characteristics like race, gender, age, sexual orientation, physical abilities, socioeconomic background, beliefs, and more. A diverse group is one with a rich mix of these qualities that brings a variety of perspectives and experiences to the table.

Inclusion is about creating an environment where a diverse mix of people all feel welcomed, respected, supported, and valued as individuals. In an inclusive workplace, differences aren't just tolerated but celebrated and leveraged. Everyone feels they can bring their whole, authentic selves to work and have equitable opportunities to contribute, grow and succeed.

Why does cultivating this diversity and inclusion matter so much? Let's look at some of the well-documented benefits inclusive organizations reap:

- **Enhanced innovation and problem-solving.** Diverse teams bring a wider range of experiences, perspectives, and thinking styles to bear on challenges. This cognitive diversity sparks more creative ideas and solutions. One study found that companies with above-average total diversity had 19% higher innovation revenues and 9% higher EBIT margins (Lorenzo et al., 2018).

- **Improved talent attraction and retention.** A reputation for inclusivity is a major draw for job seekers, especially among younger generations. Nearly half of millennials and 75% of Gen-Zers say diversity and inclusion are important factors in their job search (Shandwick, 2016). Inclusive workplaces also have lower turnover as employees of all backgrounds feel a greater sense of belonging and engagement.

- **Stronger business performance.** The most diverse companies are now more likely than ever to outperform less diverse peers in terms of profitability. Companies in the top quartile for ethnic diversity on executive teams are 36% more likely to have above-average profitability than those in the bottom quartile. For gender diversity, top-quartile companies outperform those in the bottom quartile by 25% (Dixon-Fyle et al., 2020).

- **Better reflection of customers.** As customer bases grow increasingly diverse, an employee base that reflects that diversity is better equipped to understand and serve customer needs. Inclusive teams are more likely to design products and services that resonate across markets and demographics.

- **More engaged employees.** When people feel included, they're more motivated to give their best. Highly inclusive organizations generate up to 30% higher revenue per employee than their less inclusive counterparts (Bourke & Garr, 2017). Their employees are also more likely to go above and beyond and to recommend the company to others.

Clearly, diversity and inclusion aren't just feel-good buzzwords but key levers for business success. By building an organization where a spectrum of voices are heard and valued, leaders don't just improve lives and society—they set their companies up to win.

Creating an Inclusive Culture

As a leader, one of your most important roles is to shape an organizational culture that rolls out the red carpet for diversity. You set the tone through what you say and do (or don't do) every day. Some key ways to champion inclusivity:

- **Make it a visible priority.** Weave diversity and inclusion into your company's stated values, mission, and strategy. Regularly communicate why they're important and how they tie to business goals. Your messaging shouldn't be a one-and-done box to check—it needs to be a steady drumbeat across internal and external channels that shows you're all in. Share statistics, success stories, and even areas where you're falling short and how you plan to improve. The more vocal and transparent you are, the more diversity and inclusion will stay at the top of your team's mind.
- **Model inclusive behaviors.** Your actions speak louder than your words. Visibly commit to inclusive leadership every day by seeking out and elevating diverse perspectives. Practice active listening, empathy, and cultural humility. Notice and address biased statements or behaviors. Your employees are watching how you conduct yourself to gauge how serious you are. If you advocate for

diversity but only spend time with people who look and think like you, that hypocrisy will be noted. Truly walk your inclusion talk.

- **Build diversity and inclusion infrastructure.** Make sure your organizational policies and practices support your inclusive vision. Do your hiring, pay, and promotion practices proactively level the playing field for underrepresented groups? Are your events, facilities, and communications accessible to people of all abilities? Putting equitable structures in place makes inclusion the default setting rather than an uphill battle. For example, establishing clear criteria for advancement guards against the biased "gut feeling" promotions that keep leadership homogeneous.

- **Foster an inclusion-first mindset.** Strive to make inclusive thinking become second nature for employees. Ask teams to consider inclusion impacts as part of project planning. Set the expectation that inclusive behaviors like collaboration and active listening are core to team success. The more inclusion becomes a lens applied to every decision and interaction, the more it permeates your culture. Aim for "we considered diversity and inclusion" to be a reflexive response, not an afterthought.

- **Encourage employee connection.** It's hard to nurture a sense of belonging without opportunities for authentic relationship building. Create safe spaces for people to share their experiences and perspectives through employee resource groups (ERGs), informal coffee chats, storytelling events, and more. Enable employees to learn about and appreciate different cultures, backgrounds, and identities. These meaningful conversations foster the empathy and understanding that fuels inclusion. Just be sure to set ground rules around respect to ensure interactions bring people together rather than divide them.

- **Make it measurable.** What gets measured gets done. Define diversity and inclusion goals and track metrics around representation, pay equity, turnover, employee sentiment, and more. Analyze data for insights into where you're progressing and where bias may still be creeping in. Share progress transparently to hold yourself and your organization accountable and to highlight bright spots. Tracking keeps diversity and inclusion a high priority and ensures efforts are driving real results and not just lip service.

Building an authentically inclusive culture takes consistent, visible effort from the top. When you relentlessly champion inclusion through your words and actions, you give your team explicit permission to prioritize it, too. And that opens the door to diversity and all its benefits.

Embracing Diversity of All Stripes

Inclusion is about making people of all backgrounds feel welcomed and valued. But what about when those backgrounds represent a vast array of nationalities, abilities, belief systems, and more? Honoring diversity in all its forms takes heightened cultural competency and a wider lens of inclusion. Let's unpack some key strategies.

Respect Diverse Perspectives

A major part of inclusive leadership is tuning into and appreciating the different viewpoints people bring to the table based on their unique cocktail of identities and experiences. That diversity of thought is your rocket fuel for innovation—but only if you create an environment where it's safe to share authentically.

Make respect for diverse perspectives a ground rule in your organization. When differing views inevitably arise, emphasize seeking to understand. Ask clarifying questions to better grasp where someone is coming from before rushing to judgment or consensus.

Tactfully call out interruptions, dismissiveness, or attacks that make people fearful of speaking up. The more employees trust that they'll be heard with an open mind, the more ready they'll be to voice game-changing ideas. Your example of respectful, curious engagement sets the tone.

Expand your own cultural awareness, too. If most of your team members represent a different background from your own, proactively educate yourself on their heritage, values, and norms. The more you appreciate the full context employees bring, the better you'll be able to flex your style to bring out their best.

Offer Diversity and Inclusion Training

Don't expect your teams to navigate cross-cultural dynamics intuitively. Invest in education to build their competence and confidence in inclusion. Bring in experts for in-depth training on interrupting bias, inclusive communication, ally-ship, and more.

Diversity training sometimes gets a bad rap, but a thoughtful program grounded in research and focused on practical skills can yield major mindset and behavior shifts. Bake inclusion lessons into onboarding so new hires are quickly brought up to speed. Make training something everyone at every level regularly engages in to show that growth is ongoing.

Tailor training to your company's specific diversity dimensions and needs. A tech startup with employees from a dozen nationalities and a manufacturer with an intergenerational workforce may need to focus on different nuances of inclusion. The more relevant the learning, the more likely it is to stick.

Think Beyond Accommodations

It's critical that you meet your legal requirements around equitable treatment for protected groups like people with disabilities. However, creating a playing field where everyone can do their best work often means going beyond basic accommodations to design with all needs in mind from the start.

For example, ensure any offsites are held in ADA-accessible spaces with captioning and sign-language interpretation. Provide prayer and meditation rooms. Offer benefits inclusive of same-sex partners. The more your environment and culture are set up to embrace a wide variety of identities, the less people have to exhaust energy fighting for basic needs.

This "design thinking" approach to inclusion positions differences as assets to be celebrated and leveraged rather than inconveniences to be managed. It enables you to tap the full brilliance of your diverse workforce.

Hiring and Retention Through an Inclusive Lens

Diversity and inclusion aren't an initiative owned by HR—they need to be embedded into every people process and decision. That starts before people even join your company and continues through their entire employee lifecycle. Let's look at how to build diversity and inclusion into two key talent processes: hiring and retention.

Hiring for Diversity

You can't have a culture that honors diversity if your team is homogenous. Hiring is your chance to intentionally design the vibrant mix of backgrounds and experiences you want to see represented in your company. Some key strategies:

- **Expand your sourcing.** If you're only recruiting from the same narrow pool of colleges and networks, you'll keep getting the same type of candidates. Cast a wider net by partnering with diversity-focused organizations, connecting with identity-based professional associations, and posting on job boards focused on underrepresented talent. The broader you source, the more diverse your pipeline.
- **Watch out for bias in job descriptions.** Subtle word choices in your postings could be unintentionally excluding certain groups. For example, one study found that postings with more "masculine-themed" words like "competitive" attracted fewer female applicants (Gaucher et al., 2011). Have a diverse panel review descriptions for loaded language, and aim for neutral words that invite the widest possible pool.
- **Rethink "cultural fit."** Too often, "she's a great fit" is code for "she looks and thinks just like the rest of us." Filtering for culture fit keeps you stuck in a homogeneous bubble. Instead, focus on "culture add"—the new perspectives and experiences a candidate brings that will push your thinking in a positive way. Seek to round out your culture rather than simply mirroring it.
- **Create inclusive interviews.** Again, subtle biases can creep into evaluations and skew toward keeping the status quo. Ensure a diversity of interviewers to get a well-

rounded view of each candidate. Agree on objective criteria in advance, ideally tied to a rubric or scorecard. Use structured interviews where all candidates get the same questions so the playing field is level.

Build Diversity Into Retention

Hiring diverse talent won't move the needle if those hires don't feel valued and quickly leave. Inclusion is key to holding onto your multifaceted dream team for the long haul. Some tips:

- **Create an inclusive onboarding experience.** Those early days are critical for making hires feel welcomed and setting them up for success. Share your diversity and inclusion commitments upfront. Connect new employees with mentors and invite them to join any relevant ERGs. Check that orientation activities are inclusive of different learning styles, abilities, and cultural norms. You only get one chance to make a first impression that your company walks its talk.
- **Grow careers equitably.** Lack of advancement is a top reason employees of color and women, in particular, take their talents elsewhere. Ensure your development programs and promotion processes proactively level the playing field. Use tools like a sponsorship program focused on underrepresented talent or a "bias interrupter" checklist before promotion decisions. Transparency around career growth also guards against inequities festering unnoticed.
- **Tune into the employee experience.** You can't manage inclusion if you're not regularly measuring it. Use a mix of pulse surveys, focus groups, exit interviews, and casual conversations to keep your finger on the pulse of different employee segments. Ask about their sense of belonging,

their faith in DE&I commitments, their career satisfaction, and more. Compare responses across demographics to look for themes and gaps. Really listen to that feedback to guide your continued inclusion efforts.

With an inclusive approach to hiring and managing talent, you'll be well set up to attract dynamo-diverse employees and keep them thriving for the long run. Remember, you're not just building a company for today but assembling the leadership bench of tomorrow—one that should look as multifaceted as the world you're innovating for.

The Virtual Inclusion Imperative

With more and more teams partially or fully virtual these days, inclusion takes on some new dimensions. Remote dynamics can be a great equalizer, allowing you to tap talent across geographies and accommodate a wider variety of needs. At the same time, virtual work brings risks of distance diluting your culture and leaving some feeling unseen.

Just as with in-person inclusion, leaders play a pivotal role in shaping a digital environment that works for everyone. Some strategies to consider:

- **Champion async communication.** With remote employees spanning time zones and juggling responsibilities, live meetings can't be your go-to. Defaulting to async options like email, shared docs, and Slack empowers people to engage when it fits their schedule. It also creates space for less spontaneous communicators to process and contribute. Save that precious "together time" for discussions that truly need to be live.

- **Design accessible virtual spaces.** Remote employees with disabilities or language barriers can often feel like an afterthought in virtual workspaces. Proactively design with their needs in mind by captioning videos, using dyslexia-friendly fonts, offering multiple language channels, and more. Regularly ask employees what else would help them engage fully. A "one size fits all" approach inevitably leaves some behind.

- **Create virtual water coolers.** Those spontaneous hallway chats that build rapport are harder to come by in a remote world. Be intentional about creating online spaces for employees to connect beyond projects and meetings. Consider a "life updates" Slack channel, a weekly coffee roulette pairing employees for informal video chats, or a #gratitude channel for shoutouts. These moments of human connection make people feel "seen" even through a screen.

- **Prioritize face time.** When you can't pick up on body language cues as readily, it's easy for misunderstandings and disconnects to emerge. Prioritize live video for sensitive discussions and feedback. Coach managers to do frequent video 1-1 check-ins to keep a pulse on engagement. The trust you build face-to-virtual-face creates a bulwark against your culture degrading.

- **Keep an eye on equity.** Without the visibility of an office, it's easy for inequities in experience to go unnoticed. Are certain employees consistently disadvantaged by time zone differences? Are parents unfairly burdened by live meeting times? Do team bonding activities center on a particular demographic? Regularly audit with an inclusion lens to catch disparities. An equal playing field keeps diverse remote talent in the game.

If you're not intentional about inclusion in a virtual environment, you risk gains you've made washing away with the tide of remote disconnection. The more you prioritize it in your digital tools and processes, the more you'll hold onto the benefits of diversity in the hybrid world of work.

Looking Forward

Leading diverse, inclusive organizations in our increasingly global business landscape isn't a "nice to have" but a must. Companies that fail to proactively level the playing field for all employees to contribute and succeed get left behind. Those who harness the power of diversity pull ahead of the pack.

Like any major organizational change, inclusion is a journey. It takes many small actions practiced consistently to make diversity a competitive advantage rather than a checkbox. Focus on progress over perfection. Regularly reflect on what's working, where you're stuck, and what you'll double down on or do differently moving forward. The road may be long, but the rewards are well worth it.

Some guideposts as you continue championing diversity and inclusion for the long haul:

- **Make it personal.** Nothing builds buy-in like feeling the power of inclusion firsthand. Seek out experiences that deepen your personal passion for diversity. Attend an ERG meeting for an identity group different from your own. Partner with a local community organization serving underserved populations. The more you connect to inclusion emotionally, the more energy you'll bring to embedding it in your culture.

- **Get comfortable with discomfort.** Managing diversity requires skills like discussing differences respectfully, interrupting inequitable treatment, and admitting missteps. It can feel daunting to wade into fraught topics and risk looking foolish or insensitive. Lean into that discomfort. Practice navigating charged conversations gracefully. Creating a culture where inclusion troubles are discussed honestly and productively starts with your own vulnerability and openness to growth.

- **Emphasize progress, not perfection.** Building an inclusive culture is a never-ending journey, not a destination. You will make mistakes. You will encounter thorny challenges with no clear right answers. The key is to keep learning and evolving. Celebrate small wins along the way. Be transparent about areas where you're still figuring things out. An inclusion effort that's hitting some bumps is still far better than no effort at all.

- **Make it a shared priority.** Inclusion can't be a solo crusade. The more you enroll others in championing it beside you, the more sustainable change will be. Assemble a diversity council of employees across levels to guide efforts and hold the organization accountable. Tap executives to be visible sponsors and advocates. Equip managers to be inclusion leaders within their teams. Many hands make light (and lasting) work.

- **Widen your lens continuously.** Inclusion isn't a one-and-done box to check. It's a muscle to keep strengthening as the world and your workforce change. Stay up to speed on emerging topics and evolving language around identity so you can lead in relevant, respectful ways. Keep stretching to bring in voices and perspectives you haven't heard before. The more you embrace a beginner's mindset, the more your inclusion efforts will stay fresh and impactful.

The journey toward consistently inclusive leadership is as critical as it is challenging. Creating environments where a mosaic of employees feel valued and empowered is some of the most profound work you'll do. You'll not only unleash richer innovation and performance but also play a pivotal role in chipping away at inequities that have endured for far too long.

As we close this chapter, reflect on one commitment you'll make to grow your inclusive leadership capacity and embed diversity more deeply in your culture. Perhaps it's revamping a key people process with an inclusion lens or getting more vulnerable in sharing your own experiences and missteps. Maybe it's expanding your network to build connections across differences or making a recurring calendar reminder to educate yourself on an aspect of identity. There's no action too small to start with when it comes to signaling and living your values.

Remember, this work will look different for every company and every leader. What matters most is that you step up to the plate with a learning mindset, build a shared vision, and follow through with humble, consistent effort. The ripples you set in motion will build a critical mass that redefines the future of work.

Diversity is an asset ready and waiting to be leveraged. Inclusion is a practice that all of us, whatever our identities, can commit to deepening. By growing these muscles, you won't just improve your workplace but shape a society where more and more people get to step into their light. That's the kind of leadership legacy that's well worth striving for, one brave, imperfect step at a time.

Wrapping Up

As we come to the end of our exploration of inclusive leadership, take a few moments to reflect on what you've learned. Some key themes to sit with:

- Diversity and inclusion are vital to business performance. Companies that cultivate diverse, inclusive cultures see a wealth of benefits, from enhanced innovation to stronger talent pipelines to healthier bottom lines. Inclusion isn't just a "nice to have"—it's an imperative.
- Leaders play a pivotal role in modeling and embedding inclusive practices. Through their messaging, behaviors, and decisions, leaders signal that diversity matters and empower employees to bring their full selves. They can't just talk about inclusion but must visibly live it.
- Inclusive leadership requires active, ongoing effort. There's no "easy button" or one-and-done solution for creating equitable cultures. Leaders must continuously educate themselves, evaluate policies and practices, course correct after missteps, and keep bringing in new voices. The work is never done, but always worthwhile.
- Small actions add up to big change. Building an inclusive culture happens one interaction at a time. Leaders must embrace a mindset of progress over perfection and celebrate milestones along the journey. Every step in the right direction matters.
- Reflect on how you'll apply these insights in your day-to-day leadership. What's one small shift you can commit to this week to show up more inclusively? What's an uncomfortable conversation you're ready to step into? What's an aspect of your culture you'll look at revamping

through an equity lens? Choose a starting point that resonates and build from there.

Remember, missteps and discomfort are part of the package when learning to lead more inclusively. You'll say the wrong thing sometimes. You'll feel daunted by the weight of systemic inequities. You'll question if you're cut out for this work. Keep showing up. Keep stretching. Keep championing equity even when it's hard. The world needs more leaders who are willing to get uncomfortable in the service of a more just workplace and world. You have everything it takes to be part of that vanguard.

One person at a time, one company at a time, one policy at a time—that's how we'll redefine "business as usual" to be more equitable and honor our shared humanity. Stepping up to be an inclusive leader won't just make you a more effective executive—it will equip you to be part of architecting a future where more and more people get to thrive. And that's a legacy well worth striving for with all you've got.

Case Study: Tina

Tina Kim had always been a rising star at TechCorp, a global software company. With a track record of driving results and building high-performing teams, she was tapped to lead the company's flagship product division. Tina was thrilled by the opportunity but also daunted. TechCorp had long struggled with diversity, with women and people of color underrepresented in technical and leadership roles.

As a Korean-American woman in tech herself, Tina was all too familiar with the challenges of not seeing herself reflected in company leadership. She knew that truly moving the needle on innovation would require a major culture shift to be more inclusive of all kinds of talent. She made a commitment to herself and her team that she would champion that shift.

Tina started by taking a hard look at the state of diversity and inclusion on her team. She pored over representation data, analyzed pay and promotion equity, and noted a glaring lack of diversity on her leadership bench. It was clear that despite good intentions, biases were creeping into decisions and leading to homogenous outcomes.

She knew that real change would require more than one-off initiatives. It would take embedding inclusion into every process and interaction. Tina engaged her leadership team in defining a shared vision of an equitable culture where everyone could do their best work. Together, they identified core pillars like increasing representation, equalizing access to opportunities, and fostering greater belonging.

With that strategic framework as a guide, Tina and her team got to work. They set clear diversity goals for hiring and promotions and built relationships with identity-based professional groups to tap new talent pools. They rolled out interview training and tools to help managers check bias in evaluations. Tina started holding regular office hours for candid career conversations with employees of all backgrounds to build trust and surface hidden barriers.

To equip all employees to be inclusion champions, Tina launched a training curriculum that went beyond "diversity 101" to dig into meaty topics like interrupting microaggressions and being an ally. She brought in expert facilitators to lead sessions on respectful communication across differences. All managers were expected to complete inclusive leadership workshops and teach key concepts to their teams.

Tina knew that training alone wouldn't shift behaviors, so she doubled down on modeling and incentivizing inclusion. She openly shared her own diversity learning journey and missteps along the way. In team meetings, she called out great examples of collaboration and perspective-taking. Questions about fostering equity were added to performance reviews to signal the importance of inclusion to success.

Crucially, Tina empowered employees to take the lead on many grassroots inclusion initiatives. A group of Black engineers launched an employee resource group to strengthen community and champion racial equity. A team of parents created a series on juggling work and family. A mix of LGBTQ+ employees and allies developed a playbook for gender inclusive product design. Tina made sure these groups had visible executive sponsorship and platforms to share their efforts far and wide.

Slowly but surely, Tina started to see the culture shift. Representation of underrepresented groups ticked up at all levels. Employee survey scores on belonging and psychological safety rose across demographics. Innovative product ideas bubbled up from corners that had previously stayed silent. Customers noticed that TechCorp's offerings were resonating across communities like never before.

The journey was far from over, but Tina knew celebrating milestones along the way was crucial for keeping momentum high. At the company's annual meeting, she gave out a slew of awards spotlighting inclusion and ally-ship. She shared stories of employees bringing their full authentic selves to work and driving impact. It was a visible celebration of the richness of diversity unlocked.

Looking back on that pivotal year, Tina realized leading with inclusion wasn't just good for the business—it had profoundly influenced her own growth, too. Wrestling with discomfort and embracing a beginner's mindset in conversations about identity had built her emotional intelligence. Handing the mic to a wider range of voices had sparked her creativity. Most of all, seeing the ripple effects of equity on her team filled her with a deep sense of purpose.

Tina's team still had a long way to go on their inclusion journey. But they could already see the transformative impact of a leader willing to take the reins and make diversity a core part of how they showed up every day. With each step, they were building a culture where brilliance from all backgrounds had a chance to shine—and reshaping an industry in the process.

Help Others Translate Their Vision Into Reality

Leadership is undoubtedly one of the greatest and most fulfilling challenges you will take on in your life. Few other life tasks necessitate such keen self-awareness and communication abilities. As a true leader, you not only set goals, determine roles and processes... you create an entire culture. You connect with others on a profound level, inspiring them to produce their best results while also achieving a sense of personal fulfillment.

If this book has demonstrated a thorough roadmap to becoming an effective and inspirational leader, kindly share your opinion with other readers.

LEAVE A REVIEW!

I wish you the sense of joy, pride, and satisfaction that arises when you serve as the guide who enables so many people to achieve their personal best.

Scan the QR code to leave a review:

Conclusion

In our exploration of the essential skills of exceptional leadership, you've gained a robust toolkit to elevate your impact and bring out the best in yourself and your team.

Leadership is an ongoing journey of growth requiring continuous learning, self-reflection, and stepping out of your comfort zone. Small actions, like asking thoughtful questions or having candid conversations, add up to shape culture and performance profoundly over time.

To inspire genuine followership, marry authenticity with emotional intelligence. Tune into others with empathy while staying true to your values and personality.

In our diverse, global business landscape, cultivating an inclusive environment where people of all backgrounds can thrive is a must. Model openness, practice cultural humility, and champion equity to enrich engagement, innovation, and performance.

Invest in your own well-being and support system. Make time for relationships, hobbies, rest, and reflection. Build connections with mentors, peers, and coaches for advice and encouragement.

Embrace the messiness of being human. Own your mistakes and model resilience. Stay tethered to your north star while adapting to change. Invite others along for the ride, as leadership is a team sport and a profound way to leave a legacy.

By honing the skills explored in this book, you're stepping up to meet the world's hunger for authentic, capable, caring leaders. True leadership stems from the quiet, often unsung actions you take each day to empower others and drive meaningful change.

Your leadership journey may not always be smooth, but your courage and persistence will carry you through. One conversation, one decision, one person at a time—that's how you fulfill the sacred duty of leadership and leave an enduring impact. The future is brighter with you leading the way.

References

Adams, J. Q. (n.d.). *John Quincy Adams quotes*. Goodreads. https://www.goodreads. com/quotes/584047-if-your-actions-inspire-others-to-dream-more-learn-more

Ashfaq, F., Abid, G., & Ilyas, S. (2021). Impact of ethical leadership on employee engagement: Role of self-efficacy and organizational commitment. *European Journal of Investigation in Health, Psychology and Education, 11*(3), 962–974. https://doi.org/10.3390/ejihpe11030071

Bourke, J., & Garr, S. (2017, February 28). *Diversity and inclusion: The reality gap*. Deloitte Insights. https://www2.deloitte.com/us/en/insights/focus/human-capital-trends/2017/diversity-and-inclusion-at-the-workplace.html

Dixon-Fyle, S., Dolan, K., Hunt, V., & Prince, S. (2020). *Diversity wins: How inclusion matters*. McKinsey & Company. https://www.mckinsey.com/featured-insights/ diversity-and-inclusion/diversity-wins-how-inclusion-matters

Churchill, W. (n.d.). *Winston Churchill quotes*. A-Z Quotes.https://www.azquotes. com/quote/895708

Eisenhower, D. D. (n.d.). *Dwight D. Eisenhower quotes*. BrainyQuote. https://www. brainyquote.com/quotes/dwight_d_eisenhower_109026

Emerson, R. W. (n.d.). *Ralph Waldo Emmerson quotes*. Goodreads. https://www. goodreads.com/quotes/8813163-do-not-follow-where-the-path-may-lead-go-instead

Gaucher, D., Friesen, J., & Kay, A. C. (2011). Evidence that gendered wording in job advertisements exists and sustains gender inequality. *Journal of Personality and Social Psychology, 101*(1), 109–128. https://doi.org/10.1037/a0022530

Hagberg, R. (2020, September 13). *Inspiring your team in good times and bad*. Hagberg Consulting. https://www.hagbergconsulting.com/inspiring-your-team-in-good-times-and-bad

Krosel, A. (2023, September 29). *99 inspirational leadership quotes*. Indeed Career Guide. https://www.indeed.com/career-advice/career-development/leader ship-quotes

Lorenzo, R., Voigt, N., Tsusaka, M., Krentz, M., & Abouzahr, K. (2018). *How diverse leadership teams boost innovation*. BCG Global. https://www.bcg.com/publica tions/2018/how-diverse-leadership-teams-boost-innovation

Maxwell, J. (n.d.). *John. C. Maxwell quotes*. BrainyQuote. https://www.brainyquote. com/quotes/john_c_maxwell_383606

RiverLogic. "The 20 Most Compelling Leadership Quotes To Inspire Your Team." Accessed April 25, 2024. https://riverlogic.com/?blog=the-20-most-compelling-leadership-quotes-to-inspire-your-team#

Seppälä, E., & Cameron, K. (2015, December 1). *Proof that positive work cultures are more productive.* Harvard Business Review. https://hbr.org/2015/12/proof-that-positive-work-cultures-are-more-productive

Shandwick, W. (2016, December 16). *Nearly half of American millennials say a diverse and inclusive workplace is an important factor in a job search.* PR Newswire. https://www.prnewswire.com/news-releases/nearly-half-of-american-millennials-say-a-diverse-and-inclusive-workplace-is-an-important-factor-in-a-job-search-300373675.htm

Sinek, S. (n.d.). *Simon Sinek quotes.* A-Z Quotes. https://www.azquotes.com/quote/1555541

33 Quotes to Inspire Leaders to Prioritize Diversity Now. (n.d.). InHerSight. https://www.inhersight.com/blog/diversity/diversity-quotes

TOP 25 EMPOWERING OTHERS QUOTES. (n.d.). A-Z Quotes. https://www.azquotes.com/quotes/topics/empowering-others.html

Wadors, P. (n.d.). *5 diversity and inclusion quotes for the workplace.* The Predictive Index. https://www.predictiveindex.com/blog/5-diversity-and-inclusion-quotes-for-the-workplace/

Zenger, J. P. (n.d.). *John Peter Zenger quotes.* Quotefancy. https://quotefancy.com/quote/1555169/John-Peter-Zenger-Great-leaders-are-not-defined-by-the-absence-of-weakness-but-rather-by

Conflict Resolution Guidebook for Managers

ESSENTIAL SKILLS FOR PREVENTING, MANAGING, AND RESOLVING CONFLICT IN THE WORKPLACE

Introduction

Two team leaders sit across from each other in the conference room, tension hanging thick in the air. A project deadline looms, and both are adamant their approach is the right one. The conversation escalates, leaving their colleagues anxiously looking to their manager for direction. Yet, the manager hesitates, unsure of how to mediate the growing conflict. This scenario is familiar to many workplaces, where conflict lurks in the corners of every meeting room.

The purpose of this book is straightforward: to equip managers like you with the necessary skills to prevent, manage, and resolve workplace conflicts effectively. Conflict is not just an occasional issue; it is a significant part of office life. Studies show that managers spend about 25% of their time dealing with conflicts. This affects productivity, morale, and even the bottom line. The need for effective conflict management has never been more pressing.

This book is structured around practical skills that are vital for any manager aiming to foster a harmonious work environment.

Whether you are a seasoned leader or a new manager, the insights and strategies provided here are designed to elevate your ability to handle conflicts with confidence and competence. This is not a theoretical text filled with jargon. Instead, it offers practical and applicable content that you can implement in your daily work life.

By the end of this book, you will enhance your leadership skills and improve team dynamics. You'll gain increased confidence in handling conflicts, transforming them from obstacles into opportunities for growth and understanding. These essential skills will help you build a more cohesive team, where employees feel valued and understood.

My personal motivation for writing this book stems from my own experiences in management. Early in my career, I found myself in a similar situation to the one described above. I was managing a team with diverse personalities and perspectives. Conflicts arose frequently, and I often felt overwhelmed. It was through trial, error, and learning from experienced mentors that I discovered effective conflict management strategies. This has ignited my passion for helping others navigate similar challenges.

Let's embark on this journey together, armed with the tools and insights needed to make your workplace not just a space of productivity, but a community of collaboration and respect.

ONE

Mastering Effective Communication

E very day, countless managers across the globe make a critical mistake: they hear, but they do not listen. In the midst of workplace noise, genuine communication often gets lost. Consider this - a bustling office where Jane, a project manager, is swamped with emails, phone calls, and back-to-back meetings. An employee approaches her, visibly distressed, with a conflict brewing between team members. Her mind still on the last meeting, Jane nods absentmindedly, offering quick, generic advice before moving on. The employee leaves, feeling unheard and more frustrated. This scenario plays out in many workplaces, leading to unresolved conflicts and a dip in team morale. The crux of the issue often lies in a lack of effective communication, particularly the art of active listening. This is a skill that can transform mere interactions into meaningful dialogue.

1.1 The Art of Active Listening

Active listening is more than just nodding along while someone speaks. It involves a conscious effort to understand the speaker's message, considering not just their words, but their tone, body language, and the context in which they speak. This nuanced form of communication is crucial for managers, as it fosters trust and can lead to more effective conflict resolution. When you listen with the intent to reply rather than understand, you risk missing the core issues at hand. A manager who jumps to respond may inadvertently dismiss important details, making the speaker feel undervalued. Instead, by focusing on comprehension, you can create a space where employees feel safe to express themselves, leading to more productive and harmonious workplace dynamics.

A compelling case study illustrates this principle. In a heated meeting, a manager named Tom faced two employees locked in a bitter disagreement. Instead of choosing sides or offering immediate solutions, Tom engaged through active listening. He reflected on each employee's concerns in his own words, ensuring they felt heard. By paraphrasing and summarizing, Tom not only clarified the core issues, but also defused the tension in the room. This simple act of reflection showed the employees that their perspectives were valued, paving the way for a collaborative solution. Paraphrasing and summarizing are powerful techniques that not only reinforce understanding but also validate the speaker's emotions and viewpoints.

Silence is a powerful tool often overlooked in the art of listening. By allowing a pause after a statement, you create space for deeper reflection and further elaboration. Yes, silence can be uncomfortable, but it serves as an invitation for the speaker to continue, often revealing more than they initially intended. For instance, in a team meeting, pausing after a colleague's comment might encourage them to expand on their thoughts, leading to richer discussions and new insights. Strategic silence becomes a catalyst for more meaningful dialogue, allowing you to glean insights that might otherwise remain hidden.

Avoiding common active listening pitfalls is essential for fostering effective communication. One common error is interrupting, a habit that can derail conversations and breed frustration. Another is making assumptions, which can lead to misunderstandings. Practicing patience and exercising self-restraint in meetings are crucial.

To improve your listening abilities and avoid these common mistakes, consider engaging in workshops or seminars focused on active listening, which can provide a structured environment for skill development. Role-play scenarios can be invaluable for honing these skills. By simulating real-life conflicts, managers can practice the discipline of listening without interjecting, cultivating a more patient and attentive demeanor that enhances team interactions. Feedback loops, where team members offer insights into each other's listening effectiveness, can also illuminate areas for improvement. Through practice and reflection, you will begin to transform your listening from a passive to an active skill, strengthening your leadership capabilities even further.

1.2 Assertive Communication for Clarity

Assertive communication is the backbone of clear and respectful workplace interactions. It is a skill that can transform the way you engage with your team. Assertiveness involves expressing your thoughts, feelings, and needs directly and respectfully, fostering an environment where everyone feels heard and respected. Unlike aggressiveness, which bulldozes over others to achieve personal goals, assertiveness seeks balance. It allows you to stand your ground while considering the perspectives and feelings of others. This balance clarifies your intentions and encourages a culture of mutual respect. In the fast-paced environment of modern workplaces, the ability to communicate assertively is invaluable. It empowers managers to navigate conflicts with confidence and poise, reducing misunderstandings and fostering a more collaborative atmosphere.

Developing assertive communication starts with understanding its core components. One effective framework involves crafting assertive messages that articulate your needs and expectations without assigning blame. "I" statements are particularly useful here. For example, instead of saying, "You never listen to my ideas," an assertive approach would be, "I feel overlooked when my ideas are not considered during discussions." This subtle shift in language focuses on your feelings and experiences, reducing defensiveness and opening the door for constructive dialogue. It's also crucial to clearly state your needs and expectations. Instead of vague requests, be specific about what you require and why it matters. This clarity helps others understand your perspective and sets the stage for more effective problem-solving. By consistently using these techniques, you can foster a more transparent and cooperative work environment.

However, despite its benefits, assertive communication presents challenges for many managers. One common hurdle is the fear of conflict or rejection. Many people shy away from assertiveness, worried they might upset others or face backlash. But, avoiding assertiveness can lead to passive communication, where important issues remain unaddressed, ultimately breeding resentment. Overcoming this fear requires a shift in mindset. Recognize that assertive communication is not about being confrontational; it is about being clear and honest. Building confidence in your ability to express yourself assertively can be achieved through practice and reflection. Consider why you hesitate to speak up and challenge those fears with positive affirmations or support from peers. As you gradually build confidence, you will find that assertiveness leads to more fruitful and respectful interactions.

This is another area where role-playing scenarios can offer a safe environment to practice assertiveness without the pressure of real-world consequences. Imagine a scenario where a team member frequently interrupts others during meetings. In a role-play, practice addressing this behavior assertively by saying, "I notice that interruptions are frequent, and I feel it hinders our team's ability to collaborate effectively. Can we establish a protocol to ensure everyone has a chance to speak?" This will help you refine your language and approach, making you more prepared for real situations. The role-play sessions can be organized within your team or with a mentor, providing feedback and insights to enhance your communication style. By regularly engaging in these exercises, you reinforce your ability to communicate assertively, making it a natural part of your interactions.

Assertive communication is more than a skill; it is a mindset that transforms workplace dynamics. It encourages openness, reduces conflict, and fosters a culture of respect and understanding. As you integrate these practices into your daily interactions, you will notice a shift in how your team communicates and collaborates. Assertiveness empowers you to articulate your needs clearly and respectfully, paving the way for more effective conflict resolution and stronger team relationships.

1.3 Non-Verbal Cues and Their Impact

In any conversation, what you say often carries less weight than how you say it. Non-verbal communication plays a pivotal role in reinforcing or undermining verbal messages. It's not just the words that matter; it's the posture you maintain, the gestures you use, and the facial expressions you exhibit. These elements can convey confidence or insecurity, openness or defensiveness, and they do so without a single word being spoken. Consider a manager who delivers a positive performance review while maintaining a slouched posture and avoiding eye contact. Despite the glowing feedback, their body language might suggest indifference or insincerity, leaving the employee confused and undervalued. Recognizing the power of non-verbal cues is crucial for effective communication, especially in managing conflicts where the subtleties of body language can either calm the storm or fan the flames.

To become adept at interpreting these signals, start by paying close attention to the body language of those around you. Subtle signs can speak volumes. For instance, crossed arms may indicate defensiveness, while a lack of eye contact might suggest discomfort or dishonesty. Recognizing these cues can provide valuable insights into an employee's state of mind during conflicts. You can use this awareness to tailor your approach, addressing underlying concerns before they escalate. Understanding these non-verbal signals allows you to navigate conversations with greater empathy and precision, making it easier to address and resolve conflicts effectively.

Managing your own non-verbal communication is equally important. The way you hold yourself in meetings, the expressions you wear, and the gestures you use can influence the outcome of an interaction. Open body language—such as facing the person you're speaking with, uncrossed arms, and a relaxed posture—can foster trust and encourage open dialogue. Similarly, maintaining a facial expression that conveys empathy and attentiveness helps put others at ease, making them more likely to share candidly. This openness is crucial when navigating conflicts. Practicing these skills can improve your ability to communicate non-verbally, ensuring that your actions align with your words and reinforce the message you intend to convey.

In your various role-playing scenarios, be sure to pay attention to your non-verbal communication too. Another effective method is mirror practice. This involves observing your body language in a mirror while speaking, noting any gestures or expressions that might contradict your verbal message. By becoming acutely aware of your non-verbal tendencies, you can make conscious adjustments, aligning your body language with the message you want to communicate. This practice sharpens your self-awareness, while enhancing your ability to interpret and respond to the non-verbal signals of others.

Understanding and mastering non-verbal communication is not just about avoiding miscommunications. It's about creating a workplace where messages are clear, intentions are understood, and conflicts are resolved amicably. This skill set can transform the way you interact with your team, making you a more effective and empathetic leader. As you hone your ability to read and project non-verbal cues, you'll find that your interactions become more productive, your team more collaborative, and your work environment more positive. The subtlety of non-verbal communication might seem challenging at first, but with practice and awareness, it becomes an indispensable tool in your managerial toolkit.

1.4 Managing Emotions During Conversations

Emotions often serve as the unseen force driving conversations. In conflict situations, the ability to regulate these emotions is crucial for managers. Unchecked emotions can quickly escalate a tense situation, turning a manageable disagreement into a full-blown conflict. For instance, imagine a heated discussion about project deadlines. If one person reacts with anger, the ensuing defensiveness from the other can derail any chance of a productive dialogue. Emotional regulation is not about suppressing feelings; it's about recognizing them and choosing how to respond. This skill allows managers to navigate conflicts with poise, facilitating discussions that lead to resolution rather than escalation.

Recognizing and naming emotions is the first step toward managing them. It involves pausing to identify what you're feeling and why. This self-awareness can prevent emotional reactions from clouding judgment. Consider a manager who feels frustrated during a meeting. By acknowledging this frustration, they can take a moment to breathe and decide on a calmer response. Techniques like emotional labeling, where you put a name to your feelings, can help in maintaining clarity and focus. This practice aids in self-regulation and also sets a positive example for your team, demonstrating that emotions can be managed constructively.

Maintaining emotional balance during difficult conversations requires deliberate strategies. Deep breathing exercises are a simple yet effective tool. By focusing on slow, deep breaths, you can calm your body's stress response, clearing your mind for rational thinking. Another strategy is cognitive restructuring, which involves reframing negative thoughts into more positive or neutral ones. For instance, instead of thinking, "This conflict is a disaster," you might reframe it as "This is an opportunity to find a better solution." These mental shifts can reduce anxiety and prepare you to engage more effectively in conflict resolution. These techniques empower you to remain composed, ensuring that emotional turbulence doesn't overshadow the conversation's goals.

The impact of unmanaged emotions on communication can be profound. Emotional outbursts, such as shouting or sarcasm, often lead to misunderstandings and hurt feelings, making it difficult to reach a constructive outcome. A common example is a manager who, overwhelmed by stress, lashes out at a team member. The immediate effect is a breakdown in trust and communication, with long-term repercussions on team morale. Such scenarios under-score the importance of emotional control in maintaining produc-tive workplace relationships. When emotions go unchecked, they can become barriers to effective communication, creating rifts that take significant effort to mend.

As a manager, you also play a critical role in helping others manage their emotions. Offering a calm presence can be incredibly grounding for employees in distress. By maintaining a steady demeanor, you provide a safe space for them to express their feel-ings without fear of judgment. By acknowledging their emotions and validating their experiences, you help employees feel heard and supported. Encouraging your team to adopt emotional regula-tion techniques aids in conflict resolution and also fosters a culture of emotional intelligence. When employees see their leaders model emotional control, they're more likely to emulate these behaviors, leading to a more resilient team.

Interactive Exercise: Building Emotional Awareness

Encourage your team to engage in a reflection exercise to build emotional awareness and emotional regulation. Ask team members to take a moment at the end of each week to reflect on their interactions. What emotions did they notice in themselves and others? How did these emotions influence their communication and decision-making? By consciously reflecting on these experiences, team members can develop a deeper understanding of their emotional landscape and that of their colleagues. This can help strength future conversations between team members.

1.5 Tailoring Communication for Diverse Teams

Navigating the complex landscape of a multicultural team requires more than just general communication skills. It demands a keen understanding of the cultural and individual differences that shape how messages are received and interpreted. In diverse teams, communication isn't merely about exchanging information; it's about bridging gaps between varied cultural contexts. Recognizing these differences is crucial for managers aiming to foster an inclusive workplace. Consider a team made up of individuals from different cultural backgrounds. Each member brings unique perspectives, but also distinct communication styles that can clash if not carefully managed. A one-size-fits-all approach does not work well here, making cultural sensitivity a necessary skill for any manager. Cultural sensitivity training can provide the tools needed to navigate these waters, helping managers understand and appreciate the diverse backgrounds of their team members. By honing these skills, you can create a more collaborative and productive team dynamic.

Effective cross-cultural communication requires deliberate effort and specific strategies. One fundamental approach is to avoid idioms and jargon that may not translate well across cultures. What may seem like a harmless phrase to one person can be confusing or even offensive to another. Instead, opting for clear and simple language ensures that your message is accessible to all.

Additionally, understanding communication preferences across cultures is vital. Some cultures value directness, while others may see it as confrontational. By adapting your communication style to suit these preferences, you can create an environment where everyone feels respected and understood, paving the way for more effective collaboration.

Unfortunately, misinterpretations due to cultural differences are common, often leading to conflicts that can derail team cohesion. Overcoming these hurdles require building a culture of inclusivity and respect. Encouraging open dialogues where team members can share their cultural perspectives fosters understanding and reduces the risk of miscommunication. This inclusivity enriches the team dynamic and positions the team to harness the full spectrum of ideas and innovations that diversity brings.

To support managers in developing these vital skills, there are numerous tools and resources available. Diversity and inclusion workshops offer structured environments where managers can learn about different communication styles and how to adapt to them. These workshops often include practical exercises and discussions that enhance cultural awareness and sensitivity. Language and cultural exchange programs are also beneficial. They provide managers with firsthand experience in navigating cultural differences, offering insights that can be directly applied to their teams. By participating in these activities, managers can equip themselves with the knowledge and skills needed to lead diverse teams effectively.

As you integrate these strategies into your management practices, you'll notice a transformation in how your team communicates and collaborates. The effort invested in understanding and adapting to diverse communication needs pays off in a more cohesive and innovative team environment. By prioritizing cultural sensitivity and effective cross-cultural communication, you set the foundation for a workplace where every team member feels valued and heard. This inclusive approach not only enhances team dynamics but also drives the organization towards greater success and growth. Embracing these principles ensures that you, as a manager, are well-prepared to lead in today's diverse and dynamic workplace.

TWO

Emotional Intelligence in Conflict Resolution

C onsider a typical morning at the office, where the hum of productivity is suddenly disrupted by raised voices echoing through the hallway. Two colleagues, usually amicable, are locked in a heated argument over a missed deadline. Their manager is caught off guard and watches helplessly as the situation spirals out of control. These types of scenes are common in workplaces, where emotions often run high and can lead to conflicts if not managed well. Understanding and managing these emotional undercurrents is crucial for resolving conflicts effectively. This is where emotional intelligence comes into play, offering managers a toolkit to navigate and mitigate disputes by recognizing and addressing emotional triggers.

2.1 Understanding Emotional Triggers

Emotional triggers are stimuli that elicit strong emotional reactions, often leading to conflict when unchecked. These triggers can vary widely among individuals and teams. For some, criticism might spark defensiveness, while for others, an overwhelming workload can be the tipping point. Recognizing these triggers is essential in preventing knee-jerk reactions that can exacerbate conflicts. When you identify your own triggers, as well as those of your team, you gain insight into potential flashpoints, allowing you to address issues before they escalate. This proactive approach can transform conflict from a destructive force into an opportunity for growth and understanding.

To identify personal emotional triggers, self-assessment and reflection are invaluable tools. Journaling exercises are particularly effective in this regard. By regularly documenting emotional responses to various situations, you can uncover patterns that reveal your triggers. This allows you to reflect on moments of heightened emotion, noting the circumstances and your reactions. This practice not only fosters greater self-awareness but also empowers you to take control of your emotional landscape. Additionally, seeking feedback from peers can provide an external perspective on behaviors you might be unaware of. Colleagues can offer insights into how your emotions manifest in the workplace, helping you recognize triggers that might otherwise go unnoticed.

Ignoring emotional triggers can have a profound impact on conflict dynamics. Unrecognized triggers often lead to reactive behavior, which can escalate conflicts and create a toxic work environment. Consider a manager whose stress levels spike under tight deadlines. Without acknowledging this trigger, their stress might manifest as irritability, affecting team morale and productivity. Common workplace triggers such as criticism, high workload, or a lack of recognition can create tension if left unaddressed. By bringing these triggers to light, you can develop strategies to manage them effectively, preventing them from undermining team cohesion and performance.

Managing emotional triggers requires intentional strategies to anticipate and mitigate responses. Mindfulness practices are particularly useful here. By cultivating mindfulness, you increase your self-awareness, allowing you to recognize and address triggers before they lead to conflict. Techniques such as deep breathing, meditation, or simply taking a moment to pause and reflect can help you maintain emotional equilibrium. These practices foster a sense of calm and clarity, enabling you to respond thoughtfully rather than react impulsively. By integrating mindfulness into your daily routine, you create a buffer between stimulus and response, allowing you to navigate conflicts with greater ease and effectiveness.

Interactive Exercise: Identifying Your Emotional Triggers

Grab a notebook or piece of paper to try a journaling exercise to identify your emotional triggers. Over the next week, take a few uninterrupted minutes at the end of each day to reflect on moments of intense emotion. Note the situation, your emotional response, and any patterns you observe. Consider what might have triggered your reaction and how you felt in the moment. At the end of the week, review your entries to identify common themes. This reflection will help you understand your triggers better and prepare you to manage them constructively in the future.

2.2 Self-Regulation Techniques for Managers

In the middle of a crisis, a manager's ability to maintain composure can set the tone for the entire team's response. Self-regulation, the ability to manage emotions and impulses, is a cornerstone of effective leadership. When you stay calm and collected, even in challenging situations, you think more clearly and inspire confidence in those around you. This self-control is crucial in creating a stable and productive work environment, where team members feel secure and focused, even when faced with adversity. A manager who demonstrates composure during crises can guide their team through turbulence, ensuring that decisions are made with clarity and purpose rather than under the influence of stress or panic.

There is a strong connection between self-regulation and effective decision-making. When emotions run high, judgment can become clouded, leading to hasty and often regrettable decisions. Self-regulation allows you to step back and assess situations objectively, weighing options with a clear mind. Think about a manager who is faced with a tense meeting where tempers are flaring. By maintaining composure, they can facilitate a more reasoned discussion, guiding the team toward a consensus rather than allowing the situation to devolve into chaos. This ability to stay level-headed not only enhances decision-making but also models effective conflict management for the team, fostering an environment where thoughtful deliberation is valued.

To enhance self-regulation, there are several actionable strategies you can incorporate into your daily routine.

- Breathing exercises are a simple yet powerful way to center yourself. By focusing on slow, deep breaths, you can calm your nervous system, allowing you to regain control over your emotions. Try 'box breathing', where you inhale for 4 counts, hold your breath for 4 counts, exhale for 4 counts, hold your breath for 4 counts, and repeat. This practice is particularly useful in heated discussions, where the temptation to react impulsively can be overwhelming.
- Pausing before responding gives you a moment to consider your words carefully, reducing the risk of exacerbating the conflict. The pause can also serve as a

signal to others that you are thoughtfully engaging with the situation, rather than reacting reflexively. Such mindfulness in communication can lead to more constructive dialogues and effective conflict resolution.

- Daily meditation or reflection sessions are great ways to cultivate self-regulation. Incorporate this into your practice for identifying emotional triggers. Since this practice increases your emotional awareness, by taking it one step further, you can also learn to anticipate and manage your responses more effectively. Over time, these sessions can help you develop a more balanced and resilient mindset. As you make self-regulation a habit, you'll find that your ability to navigate conflicts and make sound decisions becomes second nature, enhancing both your personal and professional life.

2.3 Empathetic Leadership in Conflict Scenarios

Empathy is the cornerstone of effective conflict resolution, acting as a bridge between differing perspectives. In its simplest form, empathy is the ability to understand and share the feelings of another. For managers, this means stepping into the shoes of employees, seeing the world from their vantage point. This connection fosters trust and openness, creating an environment where employees feel valued and understood. It is this atmosphere that paves the way for resolving conflicts amicably. Empathy is not a natural skill for everyone, but it can be cultivated through conscious effort and practice. Emotional intelligence training programs are an excellent starting point. These programs enhance your ability to recognize and regulate your emotions while understanding those of others, which is crucial in high-stress situations.

Empathetic leadership manifests in various behaviors that you can incorporate into your management style. Consider actively seeking employee input during conflicts. This means not just waiting for feedback, but actively creating spaces where team members feel comfortable sharing their thoughts and concerns. It involves asking open-ended questions and genuinely listening to the responses, acknowledging the emotions and viewpoints expressed. Acknowledging and validating team members' feelings is another critical aspect. This doesn't mean you always have to agree, but it shows respect for their perspective. Verbal affirmations like, "I can see why you feel this way," can go a long way in making employees feel valued and understood.

Developing empathy skills requires intentional and consistent practice. Take a moment and consider these few methods:

- Perspective-taking exercises - Imagine yourself in another person's situation, considering how their experiences shape their reactions. Consider reflecting with colleagues to role-play different scenarios you may have previously encountered.
- Empathy mapping exercises - Systematically analyze a person's thoughts, feelings, and actions in a given scenario. This can help gain a holistic understanding of a person's experience, helping you identify solutions that truly address the person's needs. Consider using a visual mapping method.
- Regular check-ins - These check-ins should go beyond task updates; they should be opportunities to engage in meaningful conversations about how your team members are feeling and any challenges they might be facing. Consider sharing personal stories or experiences that

relate to your team member's struggles to create a sense of camaraderie and mutual understanding.

Overall, these exercises enhance your ability to connect with others on an emotional level, making you more attuned to their needs and concerns. Over time, these practices can shift your natural response to be more empathetic, ultimately leading to stronger interpersonal relationships within your team.

Maintaining empathy in high-pressure situations can be challenging, but is crucial for effective leadership. Stress can often lead to a tunnel vision focus on results, causing leaders to inadvertently neglect the emotional needs of their team. A level of awareness enhances your empathy and fosters a more inclusive and supportive work environment. It is about creating a space where everyone feels heard and valued. When managers prioritize empathy, they lay the groundwork for a more harmonious and collaborative team dynamic. This approach resolves conflicts and also prevents them, as employees are more likely to voice concerns before they escalate.

2.4 Leveraging Emotional Intelligence for Negotiation

Imagine entering a negotiation room with the ability to read the unspoken signals of your counterpart. The subtle shift in their posture, the fleeting glance, or the tone of their voice—all offering clues to their true intentions and emotions. Emotional intelligence plays a pivotal role in negotiation, enhancing your ability to navigate these complex interactions. It's not just about knowing what to say, but understanding how to say it and, most importantly, how to listen. When you tap into your emotional intelligence, you gain a deeper understanding of the other party's needs and desires, allowing you to influence the negotiation dynamics positively. This understanding creates a space where both parties feel valued, leading to mutually beneficial outcomes. By leveraging your emotional intelligence, you can transform a potentially adversarial negotiation into a collaborative dialogue, where trust and cooperation flourish.

Applying emotional intelligence in negotiations involves several key strategies. One important technique is reading emotional cues to gauge the negotiation dynamics. Pay attention to the non-verbal signals that your counterpart is sending. Are they leaning forward, indicating engagement, or crossing their arms, suggesting defensiveness? These observations can guide your approach, allowing you to adjust your tactics in real time. Building rapport is another essential strategy. Establishing a connection with the other party fosters trust, making it easier to reach agreements. Start by finding common ground, perhaps through shared interests or experiences. This rapport eases tensions and opens the door to more honest and productive conversations. When both parties trust each other, they are more likely to collaborate, seeking solutions that benefit everyone involved.

The impact of emotional intelligence on negotiation success is well-documented. Consider this case where empathy led to a win-win solution. Two companies were at odds over a joint venture, each focused on maximizing its own gains. However, when the negotiators began to actively listen and empathize with each other's concerns, the dynamic shifted. By understanding the underlying motivations and pressures each company faced, they were able to craft a solution that addressed both parties' needs. This empathy-driven approach resulted in a partnership that not only met financial goals, but also strengthened their business relationship. This example highlights how emotional intelligence can turn a negotiation from a battleground into a platform for creative problem-solving.

Incorporating emotional intelligence into your negotiation strategy can lead to more successful outcomes. It's a skill that requires practice and reflection, but the benefits are significant. Developing these negotiation-related emotional intelligence skills goes hand in hand with developing empathy. Role-playing negotiation scenarios allows you to practice and refine your techniques in a controlled setting. These activities can also broaden your understanding of how others might feel or think during negotiations, improving your capacity to reach agreements that satisfy all parties involved. Also, by understanding and influencing your counterparts through emotional intelligence, you can navigate negotiations with greater ease and effectiveness.

2.5 Building Emotional Resilience in High-Stress Situations

In the dynamic and often unpredictable world of management, emotional resilience stands as a crucial ally. This resilience is the capacity to recover quickly from difficulties and setbacks, a trait that is indispensable in managing stress and conflict. Think of resilience as the mental elasticity that allows you to remain steady and composed, even when faced with adversity. It's not about avoiding stress or conflict, but rather about being able to bounce back and continue moving forward with clarity and purpose. This ability is fundamental for managers who must navigate the turbulent waters of workplace dynamics, ensuring they can lead effectively even under pressure.

Developing emotional resilience involves a conscious effort to strengthen your mental and emotional muscles. One effective technique is positive reframing, which involves looking at challenging situations from a different perspective. By focusing on what can be learned from a difficult experience rather than dwelling on the negatives, you can transform setbacks into opportunities for growth. This shift in mindset helps in reducing stress, while building a more optimistic outlook. Another strategy is developing a growth mindset, where challenges are seen as opportunities to learn and improve. This mindset encourages embracing difficulties as a natural part of life and work, fostering a resilient attitude. With a growth mindset, setbacks become stepping stones rather than stumbling blocks, allowing you to approach challenges with curiosity and determination.

The benefits of emotional resilience for managers are profound. Resilient managers are better equipped to perform consistently under pressure, maintaining focus and effectiveness even when the going gets tough. This will not only boost personal productivity, but also inspire confidence and stability within the team. When team members see their leader maintaining composure amidst chaos, it sets a powerful example, encouraging them to adopt a similar mindset. This ripple effect enhances the overall resilience of the team, creating a work environment where challenges are met with calmness and resolve. Emotional resilience also supports better decision-making by enabling managers to remain clear-headed and objective, even in high-stakes situations. This clarity ensures that decisions are based on rational thought rather than emotional reactivity, leading to more effective outcomes.

Incorporating resilience-building practices into your daily routine can make the development of this vital skill a natural part of your life. For instance, consider journaling about daily stressors and coping strategies. By taking time each day to reflect on the challenges you faced and how you handled them, you gain valuable insights into your resilience patterns. This reflection helps you identify areas for improvement and reinforces your strengths, boosting your confidence in your ability to cope with future challenges. Over time, this practice can deepen your self-awareness, providing a solid foundation for building emotional resilience.

Additionally, setting aside time for activities that promote relaxation and stress relief, such as exercise or hobbies, can further bolster your resilience by ensuring you have a healthy outlet for stress.

As we conclude this chapter on emotional intelligence, it's clear that these skills are not just about managing conflicts—they're about transforming how we approach challenges. Emotional resilience, self-regulation, and empathetic leadership all contribute to creating a work environment where conflicts are opportunities for growth. In the next chapter, we'll explore how to apply these skills within structured frameworks, providing you with tangible strategies to navigate and resolve conflicts effectively.

THREE

Conflict Resolution Frameworks

E nvision a dynamic workplace alive with energy, where a team of talented individuals is united by a common goal. However, just below this lively surface, tensions brew due to conflicting priorities and communication breakdowns, threatening the spirit of collaboration. The project manager, acutely aware of the growing discord, recognizes that addressing these conflicts is crucial for maintaining team cohesion and productivity. This is where the power of a well-constructed conflict resolution framework becomes evident. By systematically identifying and addressing the root causes of conflict, managers can transform potential disruptions into opportunities for growth and innovation. A structured approach resolves immediate tensions and lays the groundwork for a harmonious and resilient team.

To achieve sustainable conflict resolution, it's essential to distinguish between symptoms and root causes. Symptoms are the visible expressions of conflict—such as arguments or decreased productivity—while root causes are the underlying issues fueling these symptoms. Addressing symptoms alone may provide temporary relief, but true resolution requires a deeper understanding of the core problems. Imagine a manager dealing with frequent arguments over project deadlines. While the immediate issue seems to be time management, the root cause might be a lack of clear communication or unrealistic expectations. By identifying and addressing these foundational issues, managers can prevent future conflicts and foster a more collaborative environment.

3.1 Conducting a Root Cause Analysis

A "root cause analysis" is a powerful tool for uncovering any underlying issues. One effective method is the "5 Whys" technique, originally developed by Toyota for manufacturing, but now widely used in conflict resolution. This approach involves repeatedly asking "why" to peel back the layers of a problem, ultimately revealing the root cause. Start by clearly defining the problem statement, then ask the first "why" to explore surface-level reasons. Continue this process up to four more times, each answer leading to a more in-depth understanding of the issue. This method not only clarifies the problem, but also encourages open dialogue and transparency.

Another valuable tool for root cause analysis is the Fishbone diagram, also known as the Ishikawa diagram. This visual representation helps organize potential causes of a problem into categories, such as people, processes, or technology. By systematically exploring each category, managers can identify patterns and connections that may not be immediately apparent. This structured approach aids in uncovering root causes and facilitates a comprehensive understanding of the conflict, enabling more targeted and effective interventions. By utilizing these tools, managers can get a clear picture of the issues at hand, paving the way for meaningful and lasting resolutions.

Common root causes of workplace conflicts often stem from misaligned goals or priorities. When team members have differing objectives or lack a shared understanding of project goals, tensions can arise. Misunderstandings, whether due to unclear instructions or assumptions, can lead to frustration and resentment. To address these issues, managers must prioritize open and honest communication, creating an environment where concerns can be freely expressed and addressed. By focusing on clearly defining goals and priorities, managers can proactively prevent conflicts and create a more cohesive and productive team dynamic. Regularly check in with your team members to ensure clarity and address any questions.

Gathering information during root cause analysis is crucial for gaining insights into the conflict. Having a one on one conversations with each of the involved parties provides firsthand accounts of the issues, offering valuable perspectives that might otherwise be overlooked. These conversations should be approached with empathy and active listening, ensuring that all voices are heard and respected. Also, reviewing past conflict incidents can shed light on recurring patterns or systemic issues. By analyzing previous conflicts, managers can identify trends and develop strategies to address them effectively. This comprehensive approach not only resolves the current conflict, but also strengthens the team's ability to navigate future challenges with confidence.

Interactive Exercise: Conducting a Root Cause Analysis

To put these techniques into practice, consider conducting a root cause analysis with your team. Begin by selecting a recent conflict or challenge that has affected the team. Use the "5 Whys" technique to explore the underlying issues, encouraging open dialogue and transparency throughout the process. Then, create a Fishbone diagram to visually organize potential causes, involving team members in brainstorming and categorizing each factor. This exercise will help identify root causes, while also fostering a collaborative problem-solving mindset, empowering your team to address conflicts proactively and effectively.

3.2 Designing Resolution Frameworks

Imagine you're tasked with creating a plan that addresses an ongoing conflict and prevents future ones. This plan, or resolution framework, is a structured approach that guides you through the conflict resolution process with clarity and precision. At its core, an effective framework begins with defining clear objectives and desired outcomes. This means knowing precisely what resolution looks like—not just stopping the argument, but ensuring the team aligns on future goals. A good framework also involves stakeholder engagement strategies. This involves identifying who needs to be involved in the resolution process and understanding their interests. Whether it's team members, department heads, or even external partners, knowing who plays a part in the conflict and its resolution is crucial. Their involvement ensures that all perspectives are considered, leading to solutions that are not only fair, but also sustainable.

Creating a resolution framework requires a step-by-step approach tailored to the specific conflict at hand. Start by identifying the stages of conflict. Is it just beginning, or has it reached a peak? Different stages require different interventions. For initial conflicts, you might focus on facilitating open communication to prevent escalation. For more entrenched disputes, mediation or negotiation might be necessary. Once you've mapped out the stages, determine the appropriate interventions for each. This might include scheduled group meetings, workshops, or one-on-one discussions. Incorporating these interventions into your plan ensures that you have a roadmap to guide the conflict through to resolution. This clarity helps in resolving the current issue and equips your team with strategies to handle future conflicts independently.

Flexibility is a crucial aspect of any framework. No two conflicts are identical, and rigid frameworks can hinder resolution efforts. Instead, frameworks should be adaptable, allowing you to adjust your approach as situations evolve. For example, a conflict involving miscommunication in one department may require different tactics than a disagreement over resource allocation in another department. As the conflict progresses, new information may come to light, necessitating a shift in strategy. By building flexibility into your framework, you ensure it remains relevant and effective, regardless of the specifics of the conflict. This adaptability addresses immediate issues and also builds resilience within your team, empowering them to navigate future challenges with confidence.

Another best practice in framework development is involving diverse perspectives in the design process. By bringing together individuals from different backgrounds and roles, you gain a richer understanding of the conflict's context and potential solutions. This diversity of thought can lead to innovative strategies that might not have been considered otherwise. Additionally, engaging a broad range of stakeholders in the design process fosters a sense of ownership and commitment to the resolution. When team members feel their voices are heard, they are more likely to support the framework and its implementation. This collective buy-in is essential for the framework's success, as it ensures that all parties are aligned in their efforts to resolve the conflict.

Keep in mind, developing a resolution framework is not a one-time task. It requires ongoing assessment and refinement based on feedback and outcomes. Regularly reviewing the framework's effectiveness allows you to make necessary adjustments and improvements. This iterative process ensures that the framework remains responsive to the changing needs of your team and organization. It also provides an opportunity to learn from each conflict, using insights gained to enhance future resolution efforts. By prioritizing continuous improvement, you create a framework that not only resolves current conflicts, but also strengthens your team's ability to handle future challenges. This proactive approach fosters a culture of learning and growth, where conflicts are seen as opportunities for development and innovation.

3.3 Implementing Step-by-Step Conflict Resolution

With a conflict resolution framework in hand, the next step is to bring it to life in your organization. Implementation requires careful planning and execution, starting with clearly assigning roles and responsibilities. Each team member should know their role in the process, from mediators to those providing support. This clarity prevents confusion and ensures accountability, keeping everyone aligned with the framework's objectives. Setting timelines and milestones is equally important. These guideposts provide a roadmap for progress, keeping the team focused and motivated. By breaking the resolution process into manageable phases, you can track progress and make necessary adjustments along the way. This structured approach helps facilitate smooth implementation and builds momentum toward a successful resolution.

As you begin implementing the framework, be prepared to face potential challenges. Resistance to change is a common obstacle, often rooted in fear of the unknown or discomfort with new processes. To overcome this, fostering an environment of open discussion and support is key. Encourage team members to voice their concerns and actively address them. Transparency in the process can alleviate fears and build trust. Miscommunication among stakeholders is another hurdle that can derail progress. Maintaining clarity and consistency in communication is critical to guarantee alignment among all team members.

Regular updates among team members can help prevent misunderstandings and keep the process moving forward. By anticipating these challenges and proactively addressing them, you can navigate the implementation process more effectively. Progress check-ins also provide an opportunity to assess the framework's effectiveness and make necessary adjustments. These meetings allow you to address any issues early on, preventing them from escalating into larger problems. Feedback loops are valuable for continuous improvement. Encourage team members to provide feedback on the process, identifying areas for refinement. This feedback can inform future iterations of the framework. By incorporating these strategies, you create a dynamic and responsive conflict resolution process that can adapt to changing needs and circumstances.

Consider this case study: a multinational corporation facing a cross-departmental conflict. The company implemented a step-by-step resolution framework, starting with assigning roles to key stakeholders. Each department head was responsible for facilitating communication and collaboration within their teams. Timelines and milestones were established, with regular check-ins to assess progress. Despite initial resistance, open communication and transparency helped build trust among team members. Feedback loops allowed for continuous improvement, with adjustments made based on input from all parties involved. As a result, the conflict was resolved, leading to improved collaboration and increased productivity across departments.

This example illustrates the power of a well-executed conflict resolution framework. By assigning clear roles, setting timelines, and fostering open communication, the corporation was able to navigate challenges and achieve a successful resolution. The continuous improvement process ensured the framework's adaptability, making it a valuable tool for future conflicts. This approach not only resolved the immediate issue, but also strengthened the organization's ability to manage conflicts proactively.

As you implement your own framework, remember that it's crucial to maintain adaptability and attentiveness to your team's evolving needs, guaranteeing the approach's efficacy and longevity. To effectively evaluate the outcomes of conflict resolution strategies, employing both qualitative and quantitative methods is essential. Utilizing anonymous surveys and feedback from participants provides direct insight into the satisfaction level and areas needing improvement. Moreover, analyzing conflict recurrence rates offers a quantifiable measure of strategy success. A decrease in recurring conflicts signifies effective resolution, whereas an increase indicates areas requiring further attention. By leveraging these tools, managers can achieve a comprehensive understanding of strategy impacts and make informed decisions on necessary adaptations.

Each review is an opportunity for learning, adapting, and growing, enhancing the manager's and team's capabilities. This commitment to ongoing assessment and refinement fosters a dynamic and resilient conflict resolution framework capable of navigating modern workplace complexities, ultimately improving conflict management and team cohesion.

3.4 Ensuring Long-Term Conflict Resolution Success

Sustaining the momentum of conflict resolution efforts is a critical challenge faced by many organizations. It's not merely about resolving a single dispute; it's about embedding these practices into the very fabric of organizational culture. This means that conflict resolution should become second nature to everyone in the company. One effective strategy is to integrate conflict resolution skills into regular training programs, ensuring that both new hires and seasoned employees understand its importance. By making conflict management a core part of professional development, you instill a mindset that values proactive communication and collaborative problem-solving.

Monitoring the ongoing success of these efforts requires diligent tracking and analysis. Key performance indicators (KPIs) tailored for conflict resolution can offer valuable insights. These might include metrics such as the frequency of conflicts, the time taken to resolve them, or employee satisfaction before and after resolution efforts. Regular reporting and analysis of these KPIs help maintain focus on continuous improvement. By keeping a close eye on these indicators, you can spot trends and adapt strategies as needed, ensuring that conflict resolution efforts remain aligned with organizational goals. This systematic approach highlights areas for improvement and celebrates successes, reinforcing the value of conflict resolution within the company.

Leadership plays a pivotal role in sustaining these efforts. Leaders who commit to continuous improvement in conflict resolution set the tone for the entire organization. It's crucial for leaders to model the behavior they wish to see, demonstrating active engagement in resolution processes and supporting team members in developing their own conflict management skills. Leadership commitment should be visible and genuine, going beyond mere words to tangible actions that foster a culture of open communication and trust. When leaders prioritize conflict resolution, they empower employees to address issues constructively, leading to a more cohesive and resilient workforce.

A striking example of sustained success in conflict resolution can be seen in a tech company that made significant strides in improving employee satisfaction. Initially plagued by high turnover and frequent disputes, the company embarked on a comprehensive conflict resolution initiative. They focused on training leaders to handle conflicts effectively and encouraged open dialogue across all levels. Over time, these efforts paid off, resulting in a marked improvement in workplace morale and productivity. Employees felt valued and heard, leading to a more positive work environment where conflicts were seen as opportunities for growth rather than obstacles. This transformation was not instantaneous, but the result of a sustained commitment to integrating conflict resolution into the organization's DNA. By embedding these practices into their culture, the company resolved existing issues and built a foundation for enduring success.

3.5 Customizing Frameworks for Organizational Needs

Tailoring conflict resolution frameworks to fit the unique needs of your organization is not a luxury—it's a necessity. Every workplace has its own culture and values that influence how conflicts arise and are perceived. Understanding these nuances is key to developing strategies that resonate with your team. Customization enhances effectiveness because it acknowledges and respects the distinct identity of an organization, making conflict resolution more intuitive and less intrusive.

Different industries face unique conflict scenarios that require specialized frameworks. In healthcare, for example, conflicts might arise not just from interdepartmental issues, but also from patient care demands. Here, the stakes are high, and the repercussions of unresolved conflicts can be severe. Frameworks in such settings might incorporate protocols for patient safety and care standards, alongside traditional conflict resolution techniques. In contrast, a creative agency dealing with artistic differences might focus on collaboration and shared vision, integrating brainstorming sessions into their resolution process. Each industry presents its own set of challenges and opportunities, and frameworks should be adapted to reflect these realities. By tailoring strategies to industry-specific needs, managers can address conflicts more effectively, ensuring that resolutions are both practical and meaningful.

Customization, however, is not without its challenges. Striking a balance between standardization and flexibility can be tricky. Standardization offers consistency and clarity, which are crucial for fairness and accountability. Yet, too much rigidity can prevent the framework from addressing specific issues unique to the organization. The key lies in creating a flexible structure that allows for adjustments without losing its core principles. Also, by involving team members in the customization process, you can gather diverse perspectives that enrich the framework. This collaborative approach enhances the framework's relevance and fosters a sense of ownership and commitment among employees. When they see their input reflected in the resolution process, they are more likely to engage with and support its implementation.

An example of successful customization can be seen through the healthcare example discussed above, addressing conflicts unique to patient care environments. Faced with frequent disputes between clinical staff, the institution developed a tailored framework that integrated patient safety protocols with conflict resolution practices. This approach ensured that patient care remained the top priority while providing a structured process for resolving staff disagreements. The institution also incorporated training sessions focused on communication and empathy, recognizing the emotional demands placed on healthcare professionals. This customization not only resolved existing conflicts, but also improved overall team cohesion and enhanced patient outcomes. By aligning their framework with the specific needs and values of their organization, the institution created a sustainable model for managing conflicts in a high-stakes environment.

Incorporating customization into conflict resolution frameworks is a strategic move that recognizes the diversity and complexity of modern workplaces. It allows managers to address conflicts with precision and sensitivity, acknowledging the unique challenges faced by their teams. As you consider how to tailor your framework, keep in mind the importance of understanding your organization's culture, adapting to industry-specific needs, and balancing flexibility with standardization. By doing so, you can develop a conflict resolution strategy that is effective and will resonate with your team.

FOUR

Mediation and Negotiation Skills

E nvision an office buzzing with activity where two previously cooperative departments are now locked in a conflict over resource allocation. This standoff is causing visible strain and a decline in overall productivity. As a manager, you are tasked with the delicate role of mediator. This requires a keen understanding of human dynamics. Mediation, unlike arbitration where a decision is imposed, allows parties to reach a mutually agreeable solution through facilitated dialogue. The aim here is not merely to compromise, but to enable each individual to voice their concerns and collaboratively find a resolution.

4.1 Your Role as a Mediator

As a mediator, your role is to guide the conversation, ensuring that each party has the opportunity to voice their perspective while maintaining a focus on finding a solution. This requires active listening, thoughtful questioning, and the ability to summarize discussions effectively. As a quick refresher, active listening involves fully concentrating on what is being said rather than passively hearing the words. It's about understanding the emotions and intentions behind the words, which is crucial in defusing tensions. By asking open-ended questions, you encourage parties to elaborate on their viewpoints, uncovering underlying interests that may not be immediately apparent. This technique aids in gathering information and also in helping individuals feel heard and validated.

The mediation process begins with an initial assessment and preparation, where you gather all relevant information and set the stage for the discussion. This includes understanding the key issues, identifying the stakeholders involved, and establishing ground rules to ensure a respectful and productive dialogue. Once the groundwork is laid, you facilitate the conversation, guiding the parties through a series of discussions aimed at exploring their differences and identifying common ground. Throughout this process, your role is to remain impartial, focusing on the issues rather than the individuals. By summarizing key points and reflecting on what has been said, you help clarify misunderstandings and keep the conversation on track.

Consider this example of a manager who successfully mediated a workplace dispute. In this case, two team leaders were at odds over project priorities, each convinced that their approach was the best path forward. By employing mediation techniques, the manager created a safe space for open dialogue, allowing each leader to present their case without interruption. Through active listening and thoughtful questioning, the manager helped uncover shared goals that both leaders could rally behind. By focusing on these commonalities, they were able to devise a collaborative plan that satisfied both parties, ultimately enhancing team cohesion and project outcomes. This case illustrates the power of mediation in turning potential conflicts into opportunities for growth and collaboration.

The skills required for effective mediation are not innate but can be developed through practice and reflection. Reflective listening practices, where you paraphrase and mirror back what has been said, can significantly enhance your mediation capabilities. This shows empathy and understanding and helps clarify any ambiguities, ensuring that all parties are on the same page. By honing these skills, you can become a more effective mediator, capable of navigating complex interpersonal dynamics and fostering a more compatible workplace.

Interactive Exercise: Practicing Mediation Skills

To refine your mediation skills, we recommend a hands-on approach through role-playing exercises that mimic real workplace conflicts. Begin by partnering with a peer to enact a specific scenario where two parties are at an impasse. You and your colleague will alternate roles, each taking a turn as the mediator.

In this controlled environment, concentrate on genuinely understanding the perspectives of both sides, rather than simply waiting for your turn to speak. Use open-ended questions to delve into the core of the conflict, helping both parties to articulate their needs and concerns more clearly. This could include questions like, "What outcome would you consider fair?" or "Can you elaborate on why this issue is important to you?"

After the exercise, take time to debrief with your partner. Discuss what strategies you found effective and pinpoint areas where you felt challenged or where the conversation could have veered off course. This reflective process is crucial for converting theory into practice, allowing you to identify personal strengths and areas for growth in your mediation approach. This practical exercise not only sharpens your mediation skills, but also builds confidence in your ability to navigate and defuse conflicts constructively. By regularly engaging in these simulations, you'll enhance your competency in guiding real-world disputes toward resolution.

4.2 The Role of Neutrality in Mediation

In the intricate dance of mediation, neutrality acts as the anchor that holds the process steady. It's more than just a principle; it's the foundation upon which trust and credibility are built. Picture yourself as a mediator in a dispute where emotions are high and each party feels equally justified in their stance. Your ability to remain impartial, like a calm harbor in a storm, ensures that both sides feel heard and respected. When parties sense even a hint of bias, the entire process is jeopardized. They may perceive the mediator as an ally of the opposing side, leading to disengagement and mistrust. The risk of perceived bias can derail attempts at resolution, making neutrality not just beneficial, but crucial.

Maintaining neutrality requires deliberate effort and a clear strategy. One effective approach is to avoid language that suggests favoritism. Neutral language helps set the tone for a fair and unbiased dialogue. For example, instead of saying, "I think you should consider...", opt for, "Let's explore some options together." This subtle shift in wording places the focus on collaboration rather than directive, ensuring that your language remains even-handed. Keeping personal opinions out of discussions is equally important. It's natural to have personal thoughts about the conflict, but expressing them can undermine your neutrality. Strive to be a conduit for dialogue rather than a participant in the debate. By refraining from sharing personal beliefs, you reinforce your role as an impartial facilitator, dedicated to guiding the parties towards their own resolution.

However, it's challenging to remain neutral in all instances. Accusations of bias can arise, whether grounded in reality or perception. If this happens, it's vital to address any claims head-on with transparency and openness. Reaffirm your commitment to impartiality and invite feedback on how you can better support the process. This reassures the parties involved and demonstrates your dedication to a fair resolution. Additionally, consider enlisting the help of a co-mediator if you feel your neutrality might be compromised. Having another neutral party can lend balance to the process and mitigate any perceptions of bias. By being proactive and transparent, you can overcome the challenges of maintaining neutrality and steer the mediation towards a successful outcome.

The benefits of a neutral mediation approach are profound. When parties trust in the mediator's impartiality, they are more willing to engage openly in the resolution process. This trust creates a safe space for honest communication, allowing parties to explore their differences without fear of judgment or reprisal. It empowers parties to take ownership of the outcome, fostering a sense of collaboration and mutual respect. This empowerment enhances the likelihood of reaching an agreement and strengthens relationships, turning what could have been a divisive conflict into an opportunity for growth and understanding. Neutrality, therefore, is not merely a tool for resolving disputes; it is a catalyst for creating productive and harmonious work environments.

4.3 Effective Negotiation Tactics

Negotiation is an intricate dance, where understanding the difference between interests and positions can make all the difference. A position represents the explicit demand or outcome that one party wants, whereas the underlying interest is the true motivation behind this demand—the fundamental need or desire prompting it. Imagine two departments vying for a limited budget. One insists on funding for a new project, while the other demands resources for ongoing operations. On the surface, these positions seem at odds, but delving deeper reveals shared interests in optimizing productivity and enhancing team morale. Recognizing these interests allows for creative solutions that satisfy both parties, rather than getting stuck on rigid positions.

A robust toolkit of negotiation tactics can empower you to navigate these complex scenarios with confidence. One tool is the concept of BATNA, or Best Alternative to a Negotiated Agreement. This involves understanding your fallback options should negotiations fail. By knowing your BATNA, you gain leverage, as you're aware of the minimum acceptable outcome. For instance, if negotiating a supplier contract, your BATNA might be an alternative vendor offering similar terms. This knowledge strengthens your position and informs your strategy, enabling more confident decision-making. Anchoring techniques are another powerful tactic. This involves setting the initial terms of negotiation to frame the discussion. By establishing the first offer, you create a reference point that can influence the course of negotiations. Anchoring is particularly effective when backed by well-researched justifications, making your terms appear reasonable and well-founded.

This requires preparation before negotiating. It involves a thorough understanding of both your position and that of the opposing party. Begin by gathering relevant information and data, ensuring you're well-versed in all aspects of the negotiation. This might include market research, historical precedents, or performance metrics. Armed with this knowledge, you can anticipate counterarguments and tailor your strategy accordingly. Setting clear objectives and limits is equally crucial. Define what you aim to achieve and the boundaries beyond which you won't compromise. This clarity guides your actions and prevents concessions that could undermine your interests. With well-defined goals and limits, you can navigate negotiations with precision and purpose.

Consider a scenario where strategic anchoring secured a beneficial agreement. A tech company was negotiating a merger, with both parties initially focused on maximizing their respective valuations. By employing anchoring techniques, one party set the tone by proposing a valuation based on future growth potential rather than current earnings. This approach reframed the discussion, aligning both parties on a shared vision for growth. As negotiations progressed, they were able to craft a deal that recognized this potential, resulting in a merger that benefited both sides. This example illustrates how anchoring, when combined with a clear understanding of interests and thorough preparation, can lead to favorable outcomes.

Negotiation is a multifaceted skill that requires a blend of strategy, empathy, and adaptability. By focusing on interests rather than positions, employing a diverse range of tactics, and committing to meticulous preparation, you can enhance your negotiation effectiveness. This approach not only increases the likelihood of achieving your desired outcomes, but also fosters positive, collaborative relationships with negotiating partners. As you refine your skills, you'll find that negotiation becomes less of a battlefield and more of a cooperative endeavor, where both parties can emerge satisfied and stronger.

4.4 Finding Win-Win Solutions

In the competitive landscape of business, the notion of win-win negotiation stands out as a beacon of collaboration. This approach focuses on creating agreements that satisfy the needs of all parties involved, leading to sustainable and mutually beneficial outcomes. At its core, win-win negotiation is about moving away from the mindset of winners and losers. Instead, it embraces collaboration, where both sides work together to expand the pie rather than fight over its pieces. By prioritizing mutual gains, you lay the foundation for agreements that resolve immediate issues and build long-term partnerships. This collaborative approach fosters goodwill and trust, essential components in maintaining positive relationships.

Identifying win-win opportunities requires a keen eye for shared interests and values. One effective method is to conduct brainstorming sessions that encourage creative problem-solving. These sessions should focus on identifying common goals and exploring various solutions that address the needs of all parties. By fostering an environment where ideas can flow freely, you open the door to innovative solutions that might not have been considered otherwise. Another strategy is to delve into the underlying values and interests of each party. Understanding what truly matters to each side allows you to craft solutions that resonate on a deeper level, ensuring that each party feels their core needs are met.

Despite its many advantages, achieving win-win outcomes is no easy feat. One significant barrier is the zero-sum mindset, where parties view negotiation as a competition rather than a collaboration. This mindset can lead to rigid positions and an unwillingness to explore alternative solutions. Overcoming this requires a shift in perspective, where the focus is on collaboration rather than competition. Encouraging open communication and transparency can help break down these barriers, paving the way for more cooperative discussions. Another challenge is the additional time and energy required to reach a win-win solution. While the process may be more involved, the long-term benefits of a mutually satisfying agreement far outweigh the initial investment.

Consider this scenario, where two companies entered a partnership agreement that enhanced both their market reaches. Initially, they were at odds over resources and branding. However, by focusing on shared interests, such as expanding customer bases and increasing revenue, they were able to identify synergies that benefited both sides. Through collaborative brainstorming, they devised a joint marketing strategy that leveraged each company's strengths. This approach not only resolved the immediate conflict, but also laid the groundwork for a successful partnership that exceeded their individual capacities. This case study illustrates how win-win negotiation can transform potential conflicts into opportunities for growth and collaboration, ultimately leading to outcomes that are greater than the sum of their parts.

The path to finding win-win solutions is paved with collaboration, creativity, and a willingness to explore new possibilities. As you engage in negotiations, remember that the goal is not just to reach an agreement, but to build relationships that foster long-term success. By focusing on mutual gains and embracing a collaborative spirit, you can navigate even the most complex negotiations with confidence and poise, ensuring that all parties leave the table satisfied and empowered.

4.5 Managing Power Dynamics in Negotiation

In any negotiation, power dynamics play a crucial role in shaping the outcome. They are the invisible threads that can either bind or unravel the fabric of discussions. Power imbalances can skew negotiations, allowing one party to dominate, while leaving the other feeling disenfranchised. Picture this, where a small supplier negotiates terms with a large corporation. The corporation, with its vast resources and market influence, holds significant leverage, potentially dictating terms that serve its interests while sidelining the supplier's needs. Recognizing these power plays is essential for navigating negotiations successfully. As a manager, understanding where the leverage points lie allows you to address imbalances, creating a more equitable environment.

To manage these dynamics effectively, establishing ground rules for fairness is vital. These rules act as the framework within which all parties operate, ensuring that the negotiation remains balanced and just. Clearly defined rules might include equal speaking time or the use of a neutral third-party facilitator to guide discussions. These measures prevent dominant parties from overshadowing others, fostering an environment where all voices can be heard. Empowering disadvantaged parties to voice their needs is another critical strategy. Encourage open dialogue by creating a safe space for expression, where individuals feel comfortable sharing their perspectives without fear of retribution. This empowerment balances the scales and enriches the negotiation by introducing diverse viewpoints that might have gone unheard otherwise.

Transparency is a powerful tool in mitigating power imbalances. By sharing information equitably, you level the playing field, allowing all parties to negotiate from an informed position. Imagine a labor negotiation where management holds all the data on company finances, while employees are left in the dark. This asymmetry can lead to mistrust and resentment, undermining any potential agreement. Instead, by openly sharing relevant information, management demonstrates goodwill, building trust and encouraging collaboration. Transparency fosters an atmosphere of honesty and openness, where parties are more likely to engage in constructive dialogue, paving the way for equitable outcomes.

Navigating power dynamics requires a nuanced understanding of the forces at play and a commitment to fairness and transparency. It demands a willingness to address imbalances head-on, creating an environment where there is mutual respect. By establishing ground rules, empowering voices, and promoting transparency, you can manage power dynamics effectively, transforming potential conflicts into opportunities for collaboration and growth. In doing so, negotiations become not just a means to an end, but a process that builds stronger relationships.

4.6 Closing the Deal: Ensuring Agreement Compliance

Securing commitment to agreements is the final, yet crucial, step in the negotiation process. Without ensuring compliance, even the most meticulously crafted agreement can fall apart, unraveling the hard-earned progress made by all parties involved. The importance of follow-through cannot be overstated. It is the glue that holds the resolution together, fostering trust and strengthening relationships. When parties see that commitments are honored, trust is built, and this trust is the cornerstone of any successful, long-lasting relationship. Conversely, when promises are broken, it can lead to a breakdown in trust, making future negotiations more challenging and fraught with skepticism.

To ensure compliance, it is important to have clear documentation of the terms and responsibilities. Every agreement should be detailed in a written format, outlining the obligations and expectations of each party. This serves as a reference point that can be revisited if disputes arise, ensuring that there is no ambiguity about what was decided. Establishing timelines and checkpoints is another effective strategy. By setting specific milestones for when certain tasks or actions should be completed, you create a roadmap that guides the implementation of the agreement. These checkpoints provide opportunities to assess progress, address any issues early on, and make necessary adjustments to keep the process on track.

Monitoring and evaluation play a critical role in maintaining accountability. Regular progress reviews should be conducted to ensure that all parties are meeting their commitments. These reviews offer a platform to discuss any challenges or changes in circumstances that might affect the agreement, facilitating open communication and adaptation. By maintaining continuous oversight, you ensure that the terms are being followed and further demonstrate a commitment to the agreement's success. This ongoing engagement fosters a collaborative spirit, where all parties feel invested in achieving the desired outcomes. With this approach, you can transform a negotiated agreement into a lasting and mutually beneficial relationship.

Add Your Thoughts to the Conversation on Conflict Management

We've been exploring the pivotal role of conflict resolution skills in effective management and how these skills—such as clear communication, emotional intelligence, structured frameworks, and mediation techniques—are essential in today's dynamic and fast-paced workplace. The modern organizational landscape brings both challenges and opportunities for resolving conflict, reshaping how managers lead, collaborate, and foster a harmonious work environment.

Building conflict resolution skills isn't about achieving perfection and eliminating all disagreements. It's about equipping managers with the tools to navigate complex interpersonal dynamics, understand diverse perspectives, and foster resilience in their teams to overcome these challenges and setbacks.

At this point in your reading, I hope you've recognized how the strategies outlined in this book can lead to positive outcomes, such as enhanced team cohesion, improved productivity, and a more supportive workplace culture. If the insights and techniques in this book have made a meaningful impact on your approach to conflict resolution, you're in a great position to share these benefits with other managers and leaders.

By leaving a review on Amazon, you'll help others discover practical tools to address workplace conflicts effectively and strengthen their management skills.

Share your thoughts on this book and your own experiences applying its strategies. One of the most powerful ways to reinforce your learning is by helping others understand and apply these concepts.

Please scan the QR code to leave a review.

Thank you for your support. Together, we can demonstrate the transformative power of mastering conflict resolution skills in creating thriving, collaborative workplaces.

FIVE

Building a Conflict-Positive Culture

I magine a bustling startup where creativity flows as freely as the coffee in the break room. Yet, beneath the surface, minor tensions brew among team members, threatening to disrupt the harmony. As a manager, you recognize that these conflicts could stifle innovation and productivity if they are not addressed. The challenge lies in transforming these tensions into opportunities for growth, fostering an environment where conflict is not feared but embraced as a catalyst for positive change. This chapter explores how to cultivate a culture that views conflict as a constructive force, beginning with the cornerstone of open dialogue.

5.1 Enabling Open Dialogue

Open dialogue is crucial for effective conflict resolution. When communication channels remain open, conflicts can be addressed swiftly and constructively, preventing them from festering into larger issues. Regular team check-ins serve as the foundation for this openness, providing a structured space where team members can share updates, concerns, and ideas. These meetings, whether weekly or biweekly, create a continuous cadence of communication that keeps everyone aligned and aware of each other's challenges and achievements. Additionally, creating forums for anonymous feedback can further enhance this openness. By allowing team members to voice concerns without fear of reprisal, you encourage candidness and honesty, leading to a more transparent and cohesive team environment. These forums can be as simple as suggestion boxes or digital platforms where employees can share their thoughts discreetly.

Fostering an environment of constructive criticism requires deliberate strategies that encourage honest and respectful feedback. One effective method is the "feedback sandwich," a technique that frames criticism between positive observations. This approach softens the delivery of critical feedback and reinforces the recipient's strengths, making the feedback more palatable and actionable. Training sessions focused on giving and receiving feedback can further support this environment. These sessions equip team members with the skills to articulate their thoughts clearly and respectfully, whether delivering praise or constructive criticism. By normalizing feedback as a tool for growth rather than judgment, you cultivate a culture where continuous improvement is embraced.

Despite the benefits, maintaining open dialogue presents challenges. Fear of retribution or misunderstandings can suppress communication, leading team members to withhold their true thoughts and feelings. Building trust within your team is essential to overcoming these barriers. Trust is nurtured through consistency and transparency, demonstrating that open dialogue is valued and respected. When team members feel confident that their voices will be heard without negative repercussions, they are more likely to engage openly and honestly. Encouraging vulnerability and empathy within the team can also strengthen this trust.

By modeling vulnerability yourself—admitting mistakes, sharing your own learning experiences—you create a safe space for others to do the same.

Successful organizations have embraced open dialogue as a core component of their culture. Consider a tech company that regularly holds town hall meetings to address team concerns and gather feedback. In these meetings, leaders share updates on company progress and future plans, providing transparency and context for the team's work. They also open the floor to questions and suggestions, encouraging all employees to contribute their perspectives. This practice keeps the team informed, while also fostering a sense of ownership and involvement in the company's direction. As a result, employees feel more connected and engaged, leading to improved conflict outcomes. By adopting similar practices, you can create a culture where open dialogue is the norm, empowering your team to navigate conflicts with confidence and creativity.

Reflection Section: Open Dialogue Practices

Reflect on your current practices for fostering open dialogue within your team. Consider the following questions:

- How often do your team members have opportunities to share feedback openly?
- Are there mechanisms in place for anonymous feedback?
- What steps can you take to build trust and encourage vulnerability within your team?

Use these reflections to identify areas for improvement and develop strategies to enhance communication and openness in your team dynamic.

5.2 Strategies for Creating a Safe Conflict Space

Creating a safe space for conflict is about more than just physical surroundings; it's about fostering an environment where individuals feel secure to express their thoughts and concerns. This means cultivating both physical and psychological safety in the workplace. Physically, this could involve arranging comfortable meeting areas where team members can sit face-to-face in a neutral environment, free from distractions and power dynamics that might occur in someone's personal office. Psychologically, it involves nurturing a culture of respect and openness, where team members are encouraged to share their perspectives and listen to others with empathy. When team members feel safe, they are more likely to engage openly and honestly, which is vital for resolving conflicts effectively.

To create such a space, start by setting clear ground rules for respectful interaction. These rules should be developed collaboratively, ensuring that everyone has a say in what they entail. Typical guidelines might include listening without interrupting, refraining from personal attacks, and focusing on the issue rather than the individual. Establishing these norms helps to set the tone for discussions, making it clear that while differing opinions are welcome, disrespect is not. Another practical step is to designate neutral meeting areas for conflict discussions. These should be spaces that are comfortable and free from hierarchical implications. If unavailable, consider using virtual meeting platforms that allow participants to feel on equal footing, regardless of their physical location. Just make sure the cameras are on.

The benefits of a safe conflict space extend far beyond the meeting room. When team members feel secure, they are more inclined to participate in conflict resolution processes, leading to more robust and creative solutions. This increased willingness to engage often results in more productive discussions, as individuals feel free to share ideas and challenge assumptions without fearing negative repercussions. Furthermore, a safe space encourages a sense of ownership and accountability, as team members recognize that their contributions are valued and respected. This can lead to a more cohesive team dynamic, where conflicts are seen as opportunities for growth and innovation rather than obstacles to be avoided.

Maintaining this safety over time requires consistent effort and vigilance. Regular safety audits and feedback sessions can help ensure that the environment remains supportive and inclusive. These audits might involve anonymous surveys or one-on-one conversations to gauge how safe team members feel in conflict situations. Feedback gathered from these sessions can then inform any necessary adjustments to the ground rules or meeting practices. It's also important to continually reinforce the value of a safe conflict space through leadership actions and organizational policies. Leaders should model the behaviors they wish to see, demonstrating respect, empathy, and a willingness to listen. By consistently prioritizing safety, you can create a workplace culture where conflict is approached constructively, fostering innovation and collaboration.

Interactive Element: Safe Space Assessment

Consider conducting a "Safe Space Assessment" within your team. Invite team members to anonymously share their thoughts on how safe they feel during conflict discussions. Ask for specific examples of what contributes to their sense of safety or, conversely, what detracts from it. Use this feedback to identify strengths and areas for improvement, adjusting ground rules and meeting practices as necessary. This ongoing dialogue enhances the safety of your conflict space and empowers team members to take an active role in shaping the environment in which they work.

5.3 Conflict as a Catalyst for Innovation

Conflict and innovation might seem like unlikely companions, yet history shows us that disagreements can fuel groundbreaking ideas. Consider the invention of the airplane. The Wright brothers, driven by the challenge of human flight, faced intense skepticism and internal debates. Yet, their persistence through conflict led to a revolutionary breakthrough. Similarly, the creation of the Internet was fraught with technical disagreements, yet these conflicts pushed engineers to develop the robust systems we rely on today. In the workplace, conflict can ignite creative problem-solving. When managed correctly, it transforms tension into a platform for exploring diverse perspectives and solutions.

Leveraging conflict for creative problem-solving requires intentional strategies. One effective method is incorporating brainstorming sessions into conflict resolution meetings. These sessions should encourage all team members to voice ideas, no matter how unconventional they might seem. By fostering an environment where every suggestion is valued, you open the door to innovative solutions that might not have emerged in a more controlled setting. Diverse teams bring unique viewpoints, and when these differences clash, they can lead to creative friction. If directed constructively, this friction can result in solutions that are more comprehensive and innovative than those conceived in homogenous groups.

Changing the cultural mindset to view conflict positively involves a shift from seeing it as a disruptive force to recognizing its potential for growth. Organizations that have successfully embraced conflict-driven innovation illustrate this cultural transformation.

For example, a tech company known for its cutting-edge products attributes much of its success to its approach to conflict. Rather than stifling disagreements, it encourages open debates during development phases, viewing them as opportunities to test and refine ideas. This approach leads to better products and nurtures a culture of continuous improvement and collaboration. Employees learn to view disagreements not as personal attacks, but as critical evaluations meant to enhance their work.

This real-world scenario further demonstrates how conflict can lead to significant innovations. Take a marketing team that was struggling with a declining product line. A heated debate ensued over the direction of a new campaign. Ideas clashed, but through this conflict, a novel approach emerged. The team decided to pivot their strategy entirely, launching a campaign that tapped into an overlooked market segment. The result was a resounding success, revitalizing the product line and setting a new standard for future campaigns. This example shows how conflict, when approached with an open mind and strategic intent, can unlock new pathways to success.

To harness the potential of conflict, managers must cultivate an environment where it is safe to disagree and where diverse opinions are not just tolerated but actively sought. This involves training teams to engage constructively, focusing on ideas rather than personalities. By promoting a mindset that views conflict as a natural and beneficial part of the creative process, you can transform your team's approach to challenges. Encourage team members to bring their unique perspectives to the table, and facilitate discussions that explore the full spectrum of possibilities. In doing so, you drive innovation and build a resilient team prepared to tackle future challenges with creativity and confidence.

5.4 Training Teams for Conflict Competence

Conflict competence enables teams to address disagreements constructively, reducing tension and fostering a collaborative spirit. When team members are equipped with the skills to handle disputes, the workplace transforms into a space where differences are managed, not feared. This competence reduces workplace tension significantly, as team members learn to view conflict not as a threat but as an opportunity for dialogue and growth. It shifts the focus from avoiding disagreements to addressing them head-on, encouraging a culture of openness and resilience where challenges are met with confidence and creativity.

Developing a comprehensive training program for conflict competence requires a well-structured framework, one that encompasses the core skills needed to manage conflicts effectively. A robust program should include modules on communication, negotiation, and emotional intelligence. Communication training focuses on active listening, clear expression, and understanding non-verbal cues. Negotiation skills are crucial for finding mutually beneficial solutions, teaching team members how to balance assertiveness with empathy. Emotional intelligence training helps individuals recognize and manage their emotions and those of others, promoting empathy and reducing misunderstandings. Interactive workshops and role-playing exercises are essential components of this training too. They provide a safe environment for team members to practice and refine their conflict resolution skills, allowing them to experiment with different approaches and receive feedback in real-time. By simulating real-life scenarios, these exercises build confidence and prepare team members to apply their skills effectively in actual situations.

There are several benefits to investing in conflict competence training, that could be leveraged if you need buy in and financial support from leadership. Teams that undergo these training handle conflicts more effectively and efficiently, leading to increased collaboration and reduced resolution times. With enhanced skills, team members can address issues promptly, preventing them from escalating into larger disputes. This proactive approach saves time and strengthens team cohesion, as individuals learn to work through their differences and find common ground. Trained teams are better equipped to navigate the complexities of modern work environments, where diverse perspectives and high-pressure situations are common. They develop the resilience needed to thrive in such settings, turning potential conflicts into opportunities for growth and innovation.

Consider the example from earlier, of a healthcare team that significantly reduced patient care conflicts through targeted training. Initially, the team faced frequent disagreements over treatment plans, which affected patient outcomes and team morale. By implementing a conflict competence training program, the team learned to communicate more effectively and collaborate more closely. The training included role-playing exercises that mirrored common patient care scenarios, allowing team members to practice their skills in a controlled environment. As a result, the team became more adept at resolving conflicts quickly and amicably, leading to improved patient satisfaction and increased team morale. This success story illustrates the transformative power of conflict competence training. By investing in the development of these skills, organizations can foster a culture of collaboration and innovation.

Training for conflict competence is not just about equipping individuals with new skills; it's about embedding these skills into the team's daily practices and culture. It requires ongoing commitment and reinforcement, ensuring that the skills are continually honed and applied. Regular refresher workshops and feedback sessions can help sustain the momentum, keeping the team engaged and motivated. By prioritizing conflict competence, managers can create a work environment where differences are celebrated, and conflicts are approached with grace. This commitment to conflict competence training empowers teams to navigate challenges effectively, turning potential obstacles into stepping stones for success.

5.5 Leadership's Role in Cultivating a Positive Culture

In any organization, the tone of the workplace culture is set from the top. Leaders play a crucial role in shaping an environment where conflict is not seen as a threat but as an opportunity for growth. By leading by example, leaders demonstrate how conflicts should be approached and resolved, setting a precedent for the entire team to follow. When leaders handle conflicts with transparency and integrity, they show that open dialogue and constructive criticism are valued. This approach helps establish a norm where employees feel safe to express their concerns and ideas, knowing that their perspectives will be respected and considered. The behavior of leaders sends a powerful message about what is acceptable and expected, influencing the overall atmosphere and dynamics of the workplace.

Promoting a positive culture requires intentional actions from leaders. One effective strategy is to implement regular team-building activities that foster a sense of camaraderie and trust among team members. These activities can range from informal social gatherings to structured workshops focused on collaboration and problem-solving. By bringing the team together in a relaxed setting, leaders can break down barriers and encourage open communication. Recognizing and rewarding constructive conflict management is another crucial step. We will expand on this one in the next section (5.6), so hold this thought.

Despite the benefits, cultivating a positive culture has its challenges. Resistance to cultural change is a common obstacle that leaders must navigate. Employees may be accustomed to a certain way of doing things and may resist efforts to shift the culture. Overcoming this resistance requires patience and persistence. Leaders need to communicate the benefits of a positive culture clearly and consistently, addressing any concerns or misconceptions that may arise. Providing training and support can also help ease the transition, equipping employees with the skills and confidence needed to embrace new ways of working. Additionally, leaders must be willing to adapt their own behaviors and strategies as needed, demonstrating a commitment to continuous improvement and learning. By modeling flexibility and openness to change, leaders can inspire their teams to do the same.

There are numerous examples of leaders who have successfully fostered positive cultures within their organizations. One notable case is a CEO who transformed a company's approach to conflict through transparent communication. Faced with high employee turnover and low morale, the CEO recognized the need for change. By implementing a series of town hall meetings and open forums, the CEO encouraged employees to voice their concerns and share their ideas for improvement. This transparent approach helped identify the root causes of dissatisfaction and empowered employees to take an active role in shaping the company's future. The result was a more engaged and motivated workforce, with lower turnover rates and increased productivity. This example illustrates the transformative power of leadership in cultivating a positive culture.

As a leader, your actions set the tone for your organization's culture. By fostering a conflict-positive environment, you empower your team to embrace challenges and work together effectively. Through intentional actions and a commitment to open communication, you can create a workplace where differences are celebrated and conflicts are approached with positivity.

5.6 Celebrating Conflict Resolution Successes

Recognizing and celebrating successful conflict resolution can be a powerful tool to boost morale and motivation, cultivating a positive company culture. When employees see that their efforts to engage in respectful conflict resolution are acknowledged and appreciated, they are more likely to continue these practices. By celebrating these behaviors, leaders reinforce the importance of a conflict-positive culture and motivate others to follow suit.

Celebrating these successes can be done in creative and impactful ways. One effective method is implementing a 'Resolution of the Month' award. This award can highlight a team or individual who has demonstrated exceptional skills in managing a conflict constructively. Public recognition during team meetings or through internal communications can inspire others to strive for similar achievements. Sharing success stories in company newsletters offers another avenue for celebration. By detailing the challenges faced and the innovative solutions devised, these stories serve as inspiration and education for the entire organization. They provide concrete examples of conflict resolution in action, offering insights and strategies that others can learn from and emulate.

The impact of celebrating conflict resolution goes beyond immediate recognition. It fosters a culture of continuous commitment to resolving conflicts constructively, enhancing overall team dynamics. When employees see their efforts acknowledged, they become more engaged and willing to participate in future resolution efforts. This increased engagement translates into a proactive approach to conflict management, where team members are more likely to address issues before they escalate. Over time, this proactive mindset becomes ingrained in the organizational culture, leading to a more resilient and adaptable team. This shift improves the workplace environment and enhances the organization's capacity to innovate and grow.

Organizations that celebrate conflict successes often see significant benefits to their culture. For example, a startup known for its dynamic and collaborative environment hosts an annual 'Resolution Day' to honor team achievements in conflict management. On this day, teams come together to share their experiences, discuss challenges, and celebrate their resolutions. This event strengthens team bonds and reinforces the organization's commitment to open communication and collaboration. By creating a space for reflection and celebration, the startup cultivates a culture where conflicts are viewed as opportunities for growth and learning. This practice has contributed to the company's success, as employees feel empowered to tackle challenges head-on, knowing their efforts will be recognized and celebrated.

The practice of celebrating conflict resolution can transform how teams perceive and engage with conflicts. It shifts the narrative from one of avoidance and aversion to one of opportunity and growth. This cultural shift improves team dynamics and enhances overall organizational performance. As employees become more skilled and confident in their conflict resolution abilities, they contribute to a more harmonious and innovative workplace. This transformation is not instantaneous, but through consistent recognition and celebration, it becomes an integral part of the organizational fabric, paving the way for sustained success and growth.

SIX

Dealing with Difficult Personalities

In the vibrant ecosystem of the modern workplace, a melting pot of personalities is inevitable. Envision an office where collaboration is key, yet beneath the surface there are personality conflicts brewing. This scenario is all too common: the harshness of one team member grating against another's sensitivity, breeding a climate of discomfort. These differences can significantly impact team dynamics, leading to reduced productivity and morale. Understanding and identifying difficult personality types becomes crucial for maintaining harmony and fostering a thriving environment.

6.1 Defining Personality Types

Personality conflicts often stem from the diverse ways individuals express themselves and interact with others. While diversity enriches team perspectives, it can also lead to misunderstandings and friction. Recognizing and addressing these conflicts requires a keen understanding of the different personality types that populate the workplace. Tools like the Myers-Briggs Type Indicator

(MBTI) offer valuable insights into personality traits, helping managers better navigate interpersonal dynamics. By understanding each team member's communication preferences and behavioral tendencies, managers can tailor their approach, ensuring more effective interactions and reducing the potential for conflict.

To identify difficult personalities, managers can use observational techniques alongside personality assessments. Observing how individuals react under stress, how they communicate, and how they handle feedback provides valuable clues about their personality type. For instance, an aggressive personality may exhibit confrontational and domineering behaviors, often interrupting others and dismissing opposing views. These individuals typically thrive in competitive environments but can create tension within collaborative settings. On the other hand, passive-aggressive individuals may resist directly, using sarcasm or subtle defiance to express dissatisfaction. This indirect approach can lead to confusion and frustration among team members, as issues remain unresolved and simmer beneath the surface.

Narcissistic personalities present another unique challenge. Typically self-centered and lacking empathy, narcissists often struggle to accept criticism or responsibility. They demand admiration and can become manipulative to maintain their self-image. In the workplace, these individuals might dominate conversations, disregard others' contributions, or externalize blame. Their presence can disrupt team cohesion, as colleagues may feel undervalued or ignored. Understanding these traits allows managers to develop strategies to mitigate their impact, ensuring that team dynamics remain positive and productive.

Consider the case of a team member who consistently undermines others' contributions. This individual might take credit for colleagues' ideas or interrupt team discussions to assert their viewpoint. This behavior can erode trust and partnership, breeding resentment and disengagement. By identifying these patterns early, managers can intervene constructively, addressing the behavior and promoting a more inclusive culture. Recognizing these personality traits is the first step toward managing them effectively, reducing their potential to derail team progress.

Interactive Exercise: Personality Patterns Reflection

Take a moment to reflect on your team. Consider each member's unique personality traits and how they interact with others. Note any patterns or behaviors that stand out. Do certain individuals dominate meetings, or do others retreat when conflicts arise? Identifying these traits can help you tailor your management approach, ensuring more compatible team dynamics. This exercise encourages you to observe and understand your team, fostering a more empathetic and effective leadership style. Revisit this exercise biannually or annually to evaluate any observed changes or improvements in team dynamics and individual behaviors.

6.2 Strategies for Handling Aggressive Behaviors

Consider the impact of aggression on the workplace: it disrupts team harmony, lowers morale, and creates a hostile atmosphere. Imagine a team meeting where one member's aggressive tone silences others' contributions. This not only stifles creativity and collaboration but also instills a sense of fear and unease. Aggressive behavior can range from overt actions like shouting to subtler forms like dismissive comments or interruptions. The effects ripple through the team, eroding trust and damaging relationships. Addressing aggression is crucial to maintaining a healthy work environment. It requires a manager's steady hand to navigate these turbulent waters, ensuring conflicts do not spiral out of control.

One of the first steps in handling aggression is to remain calm and composed. This can be challenging, especially when faced with hostility, but it's vital. A composed demeanor helps defuse tension and sets a calm tone for the interaction. It signals to the aggressor that their behavior is unacceptable and won't be mirrored. Setting clear boundaries is equally important. By outlining acceptable behavior and enforcing limits, you emphasize respect and mutual understanding. When an aggressive colleague interrupts, firmly but respectfully state, "I'd like to finish my point." This not only reinforces boundaries, but also models assertive communication. De-escalation techniques, such as lowering your voice or using calm body language, can further diffuse aggressive situations. These strategies, when employed consistently, foster an environment where aggression is managed effectively.

Assertive communication is a powerful tool in addressing aggression. It involves expressing your feelings and needs clearly and respectfully, without resorting to aggression yourself. By using "I" statements, you can convey your perspective without assigning blame. For example, saying, "I feel frustrated when my contributions are interrupted," focuses on your experience rather than accusing the other person. This approach encourages openness and understanding, reducing defensiveness. Assertiveness demonstrates confidence and respect, qualities that can influence the workplace culture positively. By modeling assertive communication as a manager, you inspire others to adopt similar practices, gradually transforming the team's interaction dynamics.

This is yet another area where role-playing exercises can be invaluable for practicing these skills. By simulating confrontational meetings, managers can develop their ability to handle aggression in a controlled setting. Imagine a scenario where a team member aggressively disputes a project timeline. In a role-play, practice responding with calm assertiveness, maintaining eye contact, and using "I" statements to express your viewpoint. These exercises provide a safe space to experiment with different techniques and receive feedback on your approach. By refining your skills in these scenarios, you prepare yourself for real-world encounters, building confidence and competence in managing aggressive behaviors.

6.3 Managing Passive-Aggressiveness

Passive-aggressive behavior can be a silent disruptor. Unlike direct aggression, which is often overt, passive-aggressiveness lurks beneath the surface, undermining team cohesion and productivity. This behavior is characterized by indirect resistance and avoidance of direct communication, manifesting through actions such as procrastination, backhanded compliments, or the silent treatment. It's a confusing and frustrating dynamic that can erode trust and create an atmosphere of tension. When team members engage in passive-aggressive exchanges, the resulting ambiguity can lead to misunderstandings and a breakdown in collaboration. As a manager, it's crucial to recognize these behaviors early and address them head-on, ensuring that your team operates in a transparent and supportive environment.

Addressing passive-aggressive behavior requires a strategic approach that brings underlying issues to the forefront. Encouraging open and direct communication is a foundational step. Create an environment where team members feel safe to express their thoughts and feelings openly. This might involve setting aside dedicated time for one-on-one check-ins, where individuals can discuss their concerns without fear of judgment. During these conversations, emphasize the importance of honesty and clarity, and model these behaviors yourself. Additionally, when passive-aggressive behaviors arise, address them privately and constructively. Avoid public confrontations that can exacerbate the issue. Instead, invite the individual for a private discussion, focusing on specific behaviors and their impact on the team. This approach highlights the behavior, while opening the door for collaborative problem-solving.

Empathy plays a pivotal role in managing passive-aggressiveness. By understanding the root causes of this behavior, you can address the underlying insecurities or fears that drive it. Often, passive-aggressive individuals may feel powerless or undervalued, leading to indirect expressions of their discontent. Explore these emotions with empathy, seeking to understand their perspective and offering support. By validating their feelings and working together to find solutions, you can help them feel more secure and confident in their interactions. This empathetic approach fosters a culture of trust and openness, where team members are encouraged to communicate directly and honestly.

Consider a scenario where a manager successfully managed passive-aggressive behavior by fostering transparency and encouraging candid feedback. In this case, a team member frequently missed deadlines, offering vague excuses and deflecting blame onto others. Recognizing the pattern, the manager initiated a private conversation to explore the underlying issues. Through open dialogue, it became clear that the team member felt overwhelmed by their workload and uncertain about their role. By addressing these concerns and providing clear guidance and support, the manager was able to alleviate the individual's stress and encourage more direct communication. This intervention improved the team member's performance and strengthened the overall team dynamic, as others felt inspired to share their concerns openly.

6.4 Conflict Resolution with Narcissistic Individuals

Navigating conflicts with narcissistic individuals presents unique challenges due to their distinctive personality traits. These individuals often exhibit a strong need for admiration and a significant lack of empathy, which complicates conflict resolution. They find it challenging to accept criticism or responsibility, often deflecting blame onto others to maintain their self-image. This behavior can create a cycle of tension and frustration in the workplace, as colleagues may feel their concerns are dismissed or invalidated. The difficulty lies in the narcissist's perception of themselves as inherently superior, which can hinder constructive dialogue and mutual understanding. In a team setting, their self-centered approach can disrupt collaboration, leading to an environment where others might feel undervalued or unheard.

To effectively manage conflicts with narcissists, setting firm boundaries is critical. These boundaries must be consistent and clear, as they help define acceptable behavior and prevent manipulation. Establishing these limits provides a framework within which interactions can occur, reducing the potential for conflict escalation. It's important to communicate these boundaries assertively, ensuring that they are respected and enforced. Maintaining consistency in these interactions builds a stable environment where expectations are clear, minimizing opportunities for the narcissist to exploit any ambiguity. Additionally, focusing on facts rather than engaging in emotional arguments can prevent unnecessary power struggles. By steering conversations towards objective, data-driven discussions, you can bypass the narcissist's attempts to shift blame or evade responsibility.

Communication with narcissistic individuals requires careful navigation to avoid common pitfalls. Flattery and validation traps are tactics often employed by narcissists to manipulate situations to their advantage. While it might be tempting to use compliments to defuse tension, doing so can reinforce their behavior, leading to further challenges down the line. Instead, maintain a neutral tone and focus on the task at hand, emphasizing the importance of teamwork and shared goals. This approach redirects the conversation away from personal validation and towards collective success, aligning the narcissist's interests with the team's objectives.

Consider an example of a project lead who successfully managed a narcissistic team member by redirecting their focus towards team goals. This individual often sought recognition and dominated meetings, overshadowing others' contributions. By acknowledging their expertise in a specific area relevant to the project, the project lead was able to channel their energy into a collaborative effort. Encouraging the narcissist to take a leadership role in this context helped satisfy their need for acknowledgment while ensuring their efforts contributed to the team's success. This strategic redirection resolved the immediate conflict and fostered a more cooperative atmosphere, allowing other team members to engage more freely.

The process of resolving conflicts with narcissistic individuals requires patience and strategic thinking. It's about balancing the need to address issues directly while managing the individual's sensitivities. By establishing firm boundaries, focusing on objective discussions, and steering clear of validation traps, you can navigate these interactions more effectively. This approach mitigates potential conflicts and creates a more harmonious work environment, where all team members feel respected and valued, enabling them to contribute their best work.

6.5 Techniques for Bridging Personality Clashes

In any workplace, the tapestry of diverse personalities can be both a blessing and a curse. On one hand, diversity enriches team perspectives, offering a wide array of ideas and solutions. On the other, it can lead to misunderstandings and friction, particularly when differing personalities clash. Imagine a team where one member thrives on detailed planning while another prefers spontaneity. These differences, if unmanaged, can cause perpetual disagreements, slowing down progress. These types of situations can muddle communication, leading to a breakdown in team participation and a dip in team performance. Yet, when these differences are harnessed effectively, they can foster innovation and drive the team toward success. Managing these dynamics requires a thoughtful approach to bridge the gaps, ensuring that diversity becomes a strength rather than a source of division.

One effective technique for bridging personality differences is to organize team-building activities that highlight individual strengths. These activities not only foster camaraderie, but also allow team members to appreciate each other's unique contributions. By focusing on strengths, individuals learn to value what each person brings to the table, paving the way for more harmonious interactions. For instance, a brainstorming session where each member is encouraged to present ideas based on their strengths can illuminate the diverse talents within the team, fostering mutual respect and understanding. These activities serve as a reminder that while personalities may differ, everyone is working toward a shared goal.

Workshops on diversity and inclusion play an instrumental role in enhancing understanding and cooperation among team members. These workshops provide a structured environment where individuals can explore and discuss the nuances of different personality types, learning how to communicate more effectively across these differences. Through interactive exercises and open discussions, participants gain insights into their own biases and assumptions, equipping them with the tools to navigate complex interpersonal dynamics. By fostering a culture of inclusivity, these workshops help break down barriers, creating an environment where all voices are heard and valued. This understanding strengthens team cohesion and drives collective success by leveraging the full spectrum of team talents.

Creating shared goals is another powerful strategy for aligning diverse personalities. When team members rally around a common objective, it shifts the focus from individual differences to collective achievements. This alignment not only fosters collaboration but also reduces the likelihood of conflict, as everyone is working toward the same end. Setting clear, achievable goals encourages cooperation, as team members must communicate and coordinate to reach their objectives. This shared purpose serves as a unifying force, motivating individuals to set aside personal differences in favor of the greater good. As teams work together to achieve these goals, they develop a deeper appreciation for each other's strengths and capabilities, strengthening their overall performance.

Flexibility is crucial in managing personality clashes. This means adapting your communication style to suit different individuals, ensuring that your message resonates with each team member. For example, a detailed planner may appreciate a structured approach, while a big-picture thinker might respond better to broad concepts. By tailoring your communication to fit the audience, you can reduce misunderstandings and foster a more inclusive dialogue. Flexibility also extends to problem-solving, where being open to alternative perspectives can lead to innovative solutions. This adaptability not only eases tensions, but also creates a more dynamic and responsive team environment, where change is embraced and diversity is celebrated.

Consider the example of a cross-functional team that overcame personality differences by collaborating on shared projects. Initially, the team's varied approaches led to friction, with each member advocating for their own methods. However, by focusing on a common project goal, they learned to appreciate the unique perspectives each brought to the table. Through regular check-ins and open dialogue, they aligned their efforts, leveraging their differences to create a comprehensive and innovative solution. This successful integration enhanced the project outcome and strengthened team relationships, demonstrating the power of bridging personality clashes through shared purpose and mutual respect.

6.6 Building Alliances with Challenging Colleagues

In the workplace, building alliances can transform what might initially seem like adversarial relationships into collaborative partnerships. Challenging colleagues, often perceived as obstacles, can actually become valuable allies when approached strategically. By understanding their motivations and working styles, you unlock the potential to turn friction into synergy. This approach enhances team dynamics and leverages the unique strengths that these individuals bring to the table. By reframing these relationships, you shift the focus from conflict to collaboration, cultivating an environment where diverse ideas converge.

Developing trust and cooperation with difficult personalities requires deliberate effort and a thoughtful approach. Patience and persistence are also fundamental to building alliances with challenging colleagues. Relationships take time to evolve, and progress may be slow. It's important to remain patient, recognizing that change doesn't happen overnight. Be prepared for setbacks and misunderstandings, using them as learning opportunities rather than roadblocks. Persistence in maintaining the relationship, even when progress seems elusive, demonstrates your commitment to the alliance. Over time, this dedication can shift perceptions, transforming initial skepticism into cooperation. By consistently showing up and investing in the relationship, you lay the groundwork for a more cohesive work environment.

Consider this scenario where a manager successfully turned a challenging colleague into a project advocate. Initially, this colleague was resistant to change, often questioning new initiatives and pushing back against proposed strategies. Instead of viewing this resistance as a hindrance, the manager sought to understand the colleague's concerns and motivations. Through regular one-on-one meetings, they discovered shared interests in process improvement and efficiency. By aligning on these goals, the manager gradually won the colleague's support, transforming them into a key advocate for the project. This alliance improved project outcomes and strengthened team cohesion, as other team members witnessed the positive shift in dynamics. The colleague's insights and critical perspective proved invaluable, highlighting how alliances with challenging individuals can lead to unexpected and beneficial outcomes.

In navigating these relationships, it's crucial to approach interactions with openness and a willingness to learn. Challenging colleagues often offer unique perspectives that can enrich your understanding and approach to problem-solving. By embracing these differences and seeking common ground, you foster an environment where diverse ideas are valued and collaboration thrives. As you continue to build these relationships, you'll find that even the most challenging colleagues can become your strongest allies, driving success and growth for the entire team.

SEVEN

Legal and Ethical Considerations

In a busy workplace where operations are smoothly progressing, an unexpected silence descends as rumors of a new policy begin to spread. A manager is called into human resources (HR) to discuss a complaint that hinges on the legal nuances of workplace interaction.

7.1 Legal Boundaries in Conflict Resolution

Understanding legal boundaries is crucial for managers to navigate the complex landscape of employment law and regulations. The intricate web of legal frameworks governing workplace conflicts requires a keen understanding to ensure that actions taken are both compliant and ethical.

Employment law forms the backbone of fair workplace practices, setting clear boundaries for acceptable behavior. Title VII of the Civil Rights Act of 1964 stands as a cornerstone, prohibiting discrimination based on sex, race, color, national origin, and religion. It mandates that employers cannot discriminate in terms of work conditions, privileges, or compensation. This law ensures that all employees have the right to a workplace free from discrimination and harassment. Similarly, the Occupational Safety and Health (OSHA) Act of 1970 demands that employers provide a safe working environment, addressing issues like proper sanitary conditions and protection from workplace hazards. These laws collectively create a framework that protects employees' rights and safety, guiding managers in conflict resolution processes.

Staying within these legal boundaries is not just a matter of compliance but a safeguard against potential repercussions. Non-compliance can lead to severe legal consequences, including lawsuits, fines, and damage to an organization's reputation. Discriminatory practices, whether intentional or not, can result in significant liabilities. For example, a female crane operator faced discrimination due to inadequate sanitary facilities, violating OSHA regulations. These situations highlight the need for managers to be vigilant in upholding legal standards, ensuring that workplace policies do not inadvertently harm employees or expose the organization to legal risks.

Recognizing when legal considerations must be addressed is a critical skill for managers. Certain red flags indicate potential legal violations, such as complaints of harassment, discrimination, or unsafe working conditions. Managers should be equipped to identify these signs and take appropriate action. In cases where a harassment complaint arises, legal intervention may be necessary to protect the rights of all parties involved. Understanding the nuances of these situations allows managers to respond effectively, ensuring that conflicts are resolved in a manner that upholds both the law and the organization's values.

Consider a scenario where an employee files a complaint about a hostile work environment. The manager must navigate the situation with care, balancing the need to address the complaint while ensuring compliance with legal requirements. This involves conducting a thorough investigation, gathering evidence, and consulting with legal or HR professionals to determine the appropriate course of action. By approaching the situation with a clear understanding of the legal framework, managers can resolve conflicts in a way that protects the organization and its employees.

7.2 Ethical Decision-Making in Conflict Scenarios

Imagine a fast-paced office where decisions must be made quickly, yet fairly. As a manager, the ethical landscape is one you navigate daily, especially when resolving conflicts. Ethics in conflict resolution is not merely a guideline, but a vital component of ensuring fairness and justice. It involves balancing organizational goals with individual rights, a task that often requires walking a fine line.

To tackle ethical dilemmas effectively, a structured approach is invaluable. The PLUS Ethical Decision-Making Model offers a reliable framework. This model helps in identifying stakeholders, evaluating options, and weighing consequences, ensuring decisions align with organizational values and legal standards. By integrating ethical guidelines and codes of conduct, managers can navigate complex situations with greater clarity. These tools serve as a compass, guiding managers through the murky waters of ethical conflicts. They help in maintaining a focus on integrity and fairness, even when the path isn't clear. By adopting such a structured approach, you can ensure that your decisions reflect the core values of your organization and respect the rights of all parties involved.

Conflicts of interest can arise, particularly when decision-makers have personal stakes in the outcomes. These situations demand transparency and honesty, ensuring that personal biases do not compromise fairness. Balancing transparency with confidentiality is another common dilemma. While openness is crucial for trust and accountability, it's equally important to protect sensitive information. This balance requires discretion and judgment, ensuring that confidentiality is maintained without sacrificing the transparency necessary for collective trust. Addressing these challenges involves a commitment to ethical principles, ensuring that decisions are made with due regard for all parties involved.

Consider a situation where a manager must handle a whistleblower complaint. The ethical implications are significant, as the complaint could involve issues of fraud or misconduct. In this case, it's essential to ensure fair treatment of the whistleblower while protecting the organization's interests. This requires a careful evaluation of the complaint, maintaining confidentiality, and ensuring that the investigation is thorough and unbiased. By upholding ethical standards, the manager can navigate the complexities of the situation, ensuring that justice is served and the organization's integrity is maintained. This example underscores the importance of ethical decision-making in conflict resolution, highlighting how it leads to fair and just outcomes.

Reflection Section: Ethical Decision-Making in Practice

Reflect on a recent decision you made that involved ethical considerations. Did you use a structured model to guide your decision? How did you balance organizational goals with individual rights? Consider how you might apply the PLUS Ethical Decision-Making Model to future conflicts. Reflecting on these questions can deepen your understanding of ethical decision-making and enhance your ability to navigate complex situations.

Ethical decision-making is not just an abstract concept; it's a practical tool that guides managers in resolving conflicts with integrity. By incorporating ethical frameworks and tools into your decision-making process, you can ensure that your actions align with organizational values and uphold the principles of fairness and justice. This approach strengthens your leadership and fosters a culture of trust and accountability within your team. As you continue to engage with these ethical considerations, you contribute to a workplace environment where fairness and integrity are the cornerstones of decision-making.

7.3 Ensuring Compliance with Organizational Policies

In the realm of conflict resolution, adherence to organizational policies is pivotal for maintaining consistency and fairness. Policies serve as the bedrock upon which conflict resolution procedures are built, providing a structured approach to managing disputes. They outline the standards and expectations for behavior, ensuring that all employees are aware of their rights and responsibilities. By following these guidelines, managers can navigate conflicts with clarity, ensuring that resolutions are not only fair, but also aligned with the organization's values and objectives. This consistency fosters a sense of trust and reliability, as employees know that conflicts will be handled in a manner that is both predictable and just. When policies are adhered to, they create an environment where conflicts are less likely to escalate, as employees understand the framework within which disputes will be resolved. This understanding reduces anxiety and confusion, paving the way for more efficient and effective conflict management.

To ensure policy compliance, managers must adopt proactive strategies that integrate policy adherence into everyday conflict resolution practices. Regular policy training sessions for managers are an essential tool. These sessions provide managers with the knowledge and skills needed to apply policies consistently and effectively. They also offer an opportunity to discuss real-world scenarios, exploring how policies can be applied in various contexts. By engaging in these training sessions, managers can enhance their understanding of the policies and procedures, ensuring they are well-equipped to handle conflicts in accordance with organizational standards. Additionally, implementing checklists for policy alignment during conflict resolution can serve as a valuable resource. These checklists guide managers through the resolution process, ensuring that all aspects of the policy are considered and adhered to. By using these tools, managers can maintain a high level of compliance, ensuring that conflicts are resolved in a manner that is fair and consistent with organizational expectations.

Despite the benefits of policy compliance, challenges can arise that hinder its effectiveness. One significant obstacle is the presence of outdated policies that no longer align with the current organizational culture or industry standards. These outdated policies can create confusion and inconsistency, as managers struggle to apply guidelines that are no longer relevant or effective. To address this issue, organizations must regularly review and update their policies, ensuring they remain aligned with the evolving needs and values of the organization. Another challenge is the lack of awareness among employees and managers regarding the policies and procedures. This lack of awareness can lead to unintentional non-compliance, as individuals are unaware of the guidelines that govern conflict resolution. To combat this, organizations must prioritize communication and education, ensuring that all employees are familiar with the policies and understand their importance. By fostering a culture of awareness and understanding, organizations can enhance policy compliance, reducing the likelihood of conflicts and ensuring that disputes are resolved in accordance with organizational standards.

Consider this case study, where a conflict arises due to the misuse of email within the organization. In this case, adherence to IT policies plays a crucial role in resolving the dispute. By following the established guidelines for email usage, the manager can address the issue effectively, ensuring that the resolution is fair and consistent with organizational expectations. The policies provide a clear framework for addressing the misuse, outlining the steps that must be taken to investigate and resolve the conflict. By adhering to these guidelines, the manager can ensure that the resolution is not only compliant with organizational standards, but also fair and just for all parties involved. This adherence to policy resolves the conflict and reinforces the importance of policy compliance within the organization, signaling to employees that violations will be addressed promptly and fairly. This consistency builds trust and confidence, as employees know that conflicts will be managed in a manner that is both predictable and equitable, fostering a work environment where fairness and accountability are paramount.

7.4 Protecting Confidentiality in Disputes

Within the intricate landscape of conflict management, maintaining confidentiality is pivotal, serving as the foundation upon which trust and integrity are built. When conflicts arise, employees must feel that their concerns will be handled with discretion and respect. This assurance encourages openness, making individuals more likely to bring issues forward without fear of backlash or exposure. A workplace where confidentiality is prioritized fosters a culture of trust, allowing team members to speak candidly about problems. Without this trust, potential issues may remain hidden, festering into larger disputes that could have been resolved earlier. The act of safeguarding sensitive information is not merely about maintaining privacy; it is about creating a safe space where employees feel valued and respected.

To ensure confidentiality, specific strategies must be implemented with diligence. One effective approach is the use of confidentiality agreements. These agreements serve as formal commitments to keep all discussions and information related to the conflict private. By having parties involved sign these agreements, managers can reinforce the importance of discretion and set clear expectations. Another critical strategy is the secure handling of sensitive documents. This involves storing physical documents in locked cabinets and using password-protected files for digital information. It's essential to limit access to these documents only to individuals who are directly involved in the resolution process. By controlling who can view this sensitive information, the risk of unauthorized disclosure is significantly reduced. These measures collectively create an environment where confidentiality is not just a policy, but a practice ingrained in the organization's culture.

One of the most common issues is the accidental disclosure of information during open discussions. In meetings where multiple parties are involved, it's easy for sensitive details to be inadvertently shared. To prevent this, managers must establish clear guidelines about what can and cannot be discussed in open forums. Another challenge is the temptation to share information with colleagues out of a desire to seek advice or validation. Managers must resist this temptation and instead rely on formal channels, such as HR or legal advisors, for guidance. By doing so, they can ensure that confidentiality is upheld and trust is maintained. Managers must remain vigilant, consistently reinforcing the importance of confidentiality to prevent breaches that could compromise the integrity of the resolution process.

7.5 Documenting Conflict Resolution Efforts

A manager's day is often filled with meetings, tasks, and inevitably, conflicts. Amidst this whirlwind, the importance of documentation in conflict resolution sometimes fades into the background. Yet, thorough documentation serves as a critical pillar in managing disputes effectively, providing a clear record that supports accountability and transparency. When conflicts arise, having a documented history allows managers to trace the progression of events, understand the context, and make informed decisions. This record is indispensable, especially when legal or organizational scrutiny comes into play. Documentation protects the organization by demonstrating due diligence and serves as a historical reference, offering insights into recurring issues and patterns that can inform future strategies. By maintaining comprehensive records, managers can ensure that all parties are held accountable, reducing the likelihood of disputes reoccurring and fostering a culture of responsibility and transparency.

Creating accurate and comprehensive documentation requires a strategic approach, emphasizing consistency and attention to detail. One effective method is using standardized forms and templates. These tools provide a structured format for capturing essential information, ensuring that all relevant details are recorded consistently. By standardizing the documentation process, managers can avoid the pitfalls of incomplete or inconsistent records, which can lead to misunderstandings or misrepresentations. Key details such as dates, involved parties, and outcomes must be meticulously recorded. This practice ensures that all pertinent information is captured and also facilitates easy retrieval and analysis when needed. By maintaining detailed records, managers can quickly access the information required to address conflicts, make decisions, and implement effective resolutions. This meticulous approach to documentation enhances the overall efficiency and effectiveness of conflict resolution efforts.

Despite the clear benefits, documenting conflicts presents challenges that managers must navigate carefully. One potential issue is the risk of incomplete records. In the fast-paced environment of modern workplaces, it's easy for details to be overlooked or omitted. To combat this, managers must prioritize thoroughness, ensuring that every aspect of the conflict is documented with precision. Another challenge is the potential for biased reporting. Personal biases can inadvertently influence how conflicts are recorded, leading to skewed or inaccurate accounts. To ensure objectivity and neutrality, managers must adopt an impartial approach, focusing on factual details and avoiding subjective interpretations. By maintaining a neutral stance, managers can create documentation that accurately reflects the situation, providing a reliable foundation for resolution efforts. This commitment to objectivity strengthens the integrity of the documentation and enhances the credibility and trustworthiness of the conflict resolution process.

Consider an instance where a performance issue arises within a team. A manager records detailed observations of incidents, noting specific behaviors, dates, and interactions. This comprehensive documentation provides a clear picture of the situation, allowing the manager to address the issue effectively. By presenting an objective account of events, the manager can engage the employee in a constructive conversation, focusing on finding solutions rather than assigning blame. This approach resolves the performance issue and reinforces the importance of documentation in supporting fair and effective conflict resolution. Through detailed documentation, managers can create an environment where conflicts are managed proactively, reducing the likelihood of escalation and fostering a culture of accountability and transparency.

EIGHT

Managing Remote and Hybrid Team Conflicts

I magine an energetic virtual meeting with team members scattered across the globe. The meeting begins smoothly, but soon the screen freezes, voices overlap, and the once clear agenda becomes muddled. This scenario is all too familiar in the realm of remote work, where the absence of physical presence can lead to misunderstandings and communication challenges. As managers, you're tasked with overcoming these unique barriers to maintain effective team dynamics. In this chapter, we explore practical strategies to navigate the complexities of virtual communication, ensuring your team remains cohesive and productive despite the distance.

8.1 Effective Communication in Virtual Environments

Virtual communication presents distinct challenges. In the absence of physical cues, messages can easily be misinterpreted. A seemingly benign email might be perceived as curt or dismissive due to its tone. Without the nuance of facial expressions or body language, intentions can be misconstrued. Video call quality further complicates matters. Poor connectivity can distort voices or freeze frames, leaving participants unsure of each other's reactions or sentiments. The result is a communication landscape fraught with potential pitfalls, where even the most straightforward message can lead to confusion.

To enhance virtual communication, structured meeting agendas are essential. Clear agendas provide focus and predictability, guiding discussions and ensuring no time is wasted on tangents. Before organizing a virtual meeting, ensure there is a clear purpose and communicate it to participants. When possible, use video during calls to add non-verbal context. Seeing a colleague's smile or nod can provide reassurance and clarity, fostering a sense of connection that audio alone cannot achieve. Additionally, limit meeting invites to essential participants to maintain efficiency, aiming for no more than ten attendees. These strategies help create an environment where team members feel engaged and understood, despite the physical distance.

Clarity and brevity are paramount in virtual settings. Messages should be concise and direct, avoiding jargon or complex language that might lead to misunderstandings. When composing emails, consider the reader's perspective. Use bullet points to highlight key messages, making it easier for recipients to grasp the main points at a glance. This format enhances comprehension and respects the reader's time, allowing them to quickly absorb and respond to essential information. By prioritizing clear communication, you can mitigate the risk of misinterpretation and keep your team aligned.

Consider an example of a virtual project update meeting where visual aids played a crucial role. During the meeting, presenters used slides with a maximum of five bullet points and five words per bullet to convey complex information succinctly. This approach maintained the audience's attention and ensured that key messages were understood. By breaking down complex messages into digestible parts, presenters kept the discussion focused and productive. The meeting's success lay in its structure, demonstrating how thoughtful planning and execution can overcome the challenges of virtual communication.

Interactive Exercise: Enhancing Virtual Communication

Consider conducting a virtual communication workshop with your team. Encourage participants to practice writing clear and concise emails using bullet points, and role-play virtual meetings with structured agendas. Provide feedback on their communication style, emphasizing areas for improvement. This exercise fosters awareness and skill development, equipping your team to navigate the complexities of virtual communication with confidence.

As we delve into the nuances of managing remote and hybrid teams, remember that the key lies in adapting and evolving your communication strategies. By embracing these tools and techniques, you can foster a virtual environment where collaboration thrives and conflicts are minimized.

8.2 Addressing Miscommunications in Remote Teams

In the complex world of remote work, miscommunication stands as a formidable challenge for managers. Picture a scenario where a team member in New York schedules a meeting at 9 a.m., unaware that their colleague in Sydney will be joining at midnight. Time zone differences like these often lead to missed meetings and frustration. Without careful coordination, these variations can wreak havoc on team schedules and productivity. It's crucial to be aware of these differences and plan accordingly. Use tools like world clocks and calendar apps that automatically adjust for time zones, ensuring everyone has a clear understanding of meeting times. Clearly communicating and confirming these details beforehand can prevent unnecessary confusion and stress.

Cultural nuances in communication styles further complicate interactions. Directness in one culture might be perceived as rudeness in another, while indirect communication may seem evasive or unclear. These subtle differences can lead to misinterpretations and conflicts if not managed thoughtfully. Managers should foster an environment where team members feel comfortable expressing their communication preferences and concerns. Encourage openness about cultural norms and styles, allowing for adjustments that accommodate everyone's needs. This understanding and respect for diversity can bridge gaps and enhance communication across your team.

To address these challenges, establishing standard communication protocols is vital. These protocols serve as a foundation for clear and consistent interactions, reducing the likelihood of misunderstandings. For instance, agreeing on preferred communication channels for different types of messages—such as using emails for formal updates and instant messaging for quick questions—can streamline communication and prevent important information from getting lost. Implementing feedback loops is another effective strategy. Encourage team members to ask for clarification or provide feedback when they are unsure about a message's intent. This practice clarifies communication and empowers team members to take an active role in preventing miscommunication.

Regular check-ins play a pivotal role in maintaining alignment and reducing miscommunications. Weekly team check-ins offer a platform for discussing ongoing projects, aligning on priorities, and addressing any concerns that may arise. These touchpoints provide an opportunity to clarify goals and ensure everyone is on the same page. During these meetings, encourage open dialogue and invite team members to share updates or potential issues. This proactive approach fosters a culture of transparency and collaboration, minimizing the risk of miscommunication and promoting a cohesive team environment.

Reflection Section: Evaluating Communication Practices

Take a moment to reflect on your team's current communication practices. Are there areas where miscommunications frequently occur? Consider how time zones and cultural differences might be impacting interactions. Evaluate whether your team has established clear communication protocols and if regular check-ins are part of your routine. Use this reflection to identify potential improvements and implement strategies that enhance clarity and understanding within your team. By embracing these strategies, you can create a remote work environment where communication flows effortlessly.

8.3 Building Trust and Rapport Online

In the digital age, building trust in virtual teams is more crucial than ever. Trust is the glue that holds a team together, significantly impacting both cohesion and performance. When trust is present, team members collaborate more effectively, share ideas openly, and work towards common goals with enthusiasm. Studies consistently show that teams with high levels of trust achieve higher productivity and innovation. In a virtual setting, where physical cues are absent, this trust must be nurtured deliberately.

It requires an intentional effort to create a sense of closeness and camaraderie, even when screens and miles separate team members.

To foster trust remotely, consider incorporating virtual team-building exercises into your routine. These activities, though executed online, can effectively break the ice and encourage team members to connect on a personal level. Simple exercises like "Four Facts and a Fib" or virtual escape rooms can bring team members together, highlighting shared interests and experiences. Another powerful tool is the use of informal communication channels, such as chat groups or virtual lounges. These spaces allow team members to engage in casual conversations, share jokes, and discuss non-work-related topics, much like they would in an office break room. These interactions build rapport, humanize team members, and create an environment where employees feel comfortable and valued.

Regular one-on-one meetings are another strategy to build trust and understanding. These sessions provide an opportunity to address individual concerns, offer personalized feedback, and discuss career development. By taking the time to understand each team member's unique challenges and aspirations, you demonstrate genuine care and investment in their success. These meetings are a chance to listen, to offer support, and to build a deeper connection that transcends the virtual divide. They also allow you to gain insights into team dynamics and identify potential issues before they escalate into conflicts.

Initial skepticism is common, especially among new team members who have not yet had the chance to build personal connections. Overcoming this skepticism requires consistency and transparency. Be open about your intentions and encourage team members to do the same. Share your own experiences and encourage others to share theirs. This openness can create a foundation of trust that grows stronger over time. It's important to be patient and persistent, as building trust is a gradual process that requires continuous effort and reinforcement.

Consider the example of a distributed team that organized virtual coffee breaks to enhance camaraderie. These informal gatherings provided a space for team members to chat about their weekends, discuss hobbies, or simply enjoy a cup of coffee together. Over time, these moments of connection fostered a sense of belonging and trust, transforming the team dynamics. Team members felt more comfortable reaching out for help, collaborating on projects, and sharing their ideas. The virtual coffee breaks, though simple, laid the groundwork for a cohesive and supportive team environment. This initiative illustrates how creativity and intentionality in building rapport can lead to meaningful connections, even in a virtual world.

8.4 Strategies for Remote Conflict Mediation

Mediating conflicts in a remote setting presents unique challenges and opportunities for managers. Without the benefit of face-to-face interaction, traditional mediation skills require adaptation to a virtual environment. However, the core principles of mediation remain unchanged: facilitating communication, fostering understanding, and guiding conflicting parties towards a mutually agreeable solution. In a virtual setting, the role of a neutral facilitator becomes even more critical. The facilitator acts as an impartial guide who ensures that both parties have the opportunity to express their perspectives. This neutrality helps maintain balance, encourages open dialogue, and fosters trust between all participants. By embracing technology, managers can create a structured and effective mediation environment that mirrors the success of in-person interactions.

A step-by-step guide for conducting remote mediation begins with thorough preparation. Prior to the mediation session, gather information through pre-meeting surveys. These surveys allow each party to express their concerns, identify key issues, and set expectations for the mediation process. This preparation helps the facilitator understand the conflict's dynamics and anticipate potential areas of agreement or contention. Next, establish clear ground rules for the virtual mediation session. Ensure that all participants understand and agree to these rules, which may include guidelines for respectful communication, equal speaking time, and confidentiality. By setting the stage for a respectful and focused discussion, these rules create a safe and productive environment for conflict resolution.

Technology plays a vital role in remote mediation by providing tools that enhance communication and maintain accountability. Breakout rooms, a feature available on many video conferencing platforms, allow for private discussions between the mediator and individual parties. These sessions provide a space for participants to speak candidly and explore sensitive topics without the pressure of a group setting. Additionally, recording the mediation session can serve as a valuable tool for accountability and review. It allows parties to revisit the discussions and agreements, ensuring that all commitments are clear and understood. However, it is essential to obtain consent from all participants before recording, as this practice must align with privacy considerations and legal requirements.

Successful remote mediation can be illustrated through the example of a customer service team resolving a dispute over resource allocation. The conflict arose when different departments competed for limited resources, leading to frustration and tension. The manager initiated a virtual mediation session, beginning with pre-meeting surveys to gather each department's perspectives and concerns. During the mediation, the manager facilitated a structured discussion, allowing each party to articulate their needs and proposed solutions. Breakout rooms provided a space for private conversations, where individuals could express sensitive issues without fear of judgment. Through open communication and mutual understanding, the parties reached a consensus on resource allocation that satisfied all involved. The mediation resolved the immediate conflict and strengthened interdepartmental relationships, fostering collaboration for future projects.

In conducting remote mediation, managers must remain adaptable, responsive, and committed to creating a fair and open dialogue. By leveraging technology and adhering to structured processes, you can guide your team through conflicts with confidence, transforming challenges into opportunities for growth and understanding.

8.5 Technology Tools for Conflict Management

Digital tools facilitate communication and help with conflict resolution, offering a structured approach to track and manage disagreements. Software that welcomes collaboration stands out as a game-changer, particularly for conflict tracking. These platforms allow managers to record and monitor the progress of conflict resolution efforts, ensuring that nothing slips through the cracks. With features that enable document sharing, task assignment, and real-time updates, collaboration tools provide a transparent space where team members can see the status of ongoing conflicts. This transparency is crucial for maintaining accountability and ensuring that everyone is on the same page, reducing the chances of misunderstandings or unresolved issues festering over time. Furthermore, by centralizing communication and documentation, these tools streamline the conflict resolution process, allowing managers to focus on finding solutions rather than getting bogged down in administrative details.

A variety of technology tools are available to aid in conflict management, each designed to address specific needs within a team. Platforms like Slack and Microsoft Teams facilitate real-time communication, offering channels where team members can discuss issues as they arise. These tools provide a space for quick exchanges and immediate feedback, helping to resolve minor conflicts before they escalate. For task tracking, project management tools such as Trello or Asana are invaluable. They allow managers to assign tasks related to conflict resolution, set deadlines, and monitor progress. This organized approach ensures that all parties involved understand their responsibilities and can work towards resolution efficiently. The visual nature of these platforms, with boards and cards representing different tasks, makes it easy for everyone to see the big picture and their role within it. By integrating these tools into daily operations, managers can create a more structured and proactive approach to conflict management.

Choosing the right tools for your team is a critical step in leveraging technology effectively. It's essential to select tools that align with your team's size, needs, and the complexity of tasks you undertake. For smaller teams, a simple communication app might suffice, while larger teams with more intricate needs might benefit from a robust project management system. Evaluate each tool based on its features, ease of use, and integration capabilities with other software your team already uses. Consider conducting a needs assessment to determine which tools will best support your team's conflict management efforts. This assessment should involve input from team members to ensure that the chosen tools meet their needs and preferences. By carefully selecting tools that fit your team's dynamics, you can enhance communication, streamline workflows, and ultimately improve your team's ability to manage conflicts effectively.

Consider a scenario where a marketing team utilized a shared document platform to collaborate on campaign strategies. The team, spread across different locations, faced challenges in coordinating their efforts and sharing ideas. By using a centralized platform, they could upload documents, provide feedback, and make real-time edits, all within a single interface. This open access to information allowed team members to stay informed about each other's contributions, minimizing misunderstandings and fostering a sense of unity. The platform also included a comment feature, enabling team members to discuss potential conflicts directly on the document, ensuring that issues were addressed promptly. As a result, the team successfully launched a cohesive campaign that reflected diverse perspectives and expertise. This example highlights the transformative power of technology in managing remote conflicts, showcasing how the right tools can bridge gaps and facilitate effective collaboration.

A Chance to Pay It Forward

As you turn the last pages of this book, please take a moment to hold the door open for someone else – for another manager that may be experiencing conflicts with their team.

Simply by sharing one or two sentences about your own experiences with conflict resolution, you'll show new readers where they can find the tools they need to build stronger, more cohesive teams.

Please scan the QR code to leave a review.

Thank you for your support. We're all on our own leadership journey, but every bit of insight we share can make a significant impact on shaping healthier, more collaborative workplaces.

Conclusion

As we reach the end of this book, I hope that the journey we've embarked on together has been insightful and empowering. The primary goal of this book was to equip you, as a manager, with practical skills to prevent, manage, and resolve conflicts in the workplace. Conflict is an inevitable part of any professional environment, but with the right tools and mindset, it can be transformed into an opportunity for growth, collaboration, and innovation.

Throughout the chapters, we've delved into different aspects of conflict management. We began with the foundation of effective communication, emphasizing the power of active listening, empathy, and assertive communication. These skills are crucial in understanding and addressing the needs of your team, ensuring that everyone feels heard and respected.

We then explored the realm of emotional intelligence, a vital component in recognizing and managing emotions during conflicts. By understanding emotional triggers and practicing self-regulation, you can maintain composure and guide your team through challenging situations with empathy and clarity.

Followed by structured conflict resolution frameworks, offering you a step-by-step approach to identifying root causes and implementing effective solutions. These frameworks are designed to provide clarity and consistency, ensuring that conflicts are addressed systematically and fairly.

Mediation and negotiation skills were also highlighted, showing how you can facilitate discussions and find win-win solutions. By maintaining neutrality and focusing on shared interests, you can foster a collaborative environment where conflicts become opportunities for creative problem-solving.

Building a conflict-positive culture was another key focus, encouraging open dialogue and constructive criticism. This culture enhances team dynamics and drives innovation by leveraging diverse perspectives.

When dealing with difficult personalities, we provided strategies to manage and resolve conflicts with tact and understanding. Recognizing different personality types and adapting your approach can transform potential adversities into productive relationships.

Finally, we addressed legal and ethical considerations, ensuring that your conflict management practices align with organizational policies and legal standards. This ensures compliance and fosters a workplace that upholds fairness and integrity.

The key takeaway for you as a manager is that conflict management is a multifaceted skill set. It's not just about resolving disputes—it's about leading with empathy, fostering a positive culture, and turning challenges into opportunities for growth. By applying the skills and strategies discussed, you can enhance your leadership capabilities, improve team cohesion, and drive professional development in your organization.

I encourage you to take action. Reflect on what you've learned and implement these strategies in your daily interactions. Practice active listening, embrace diversity, and lead with empathy. Your role as a manager is pivotal in creating a harmonious and productive work environment. I hope that the insights shared here will have a lasting impact on you and your team.

Remember, conflict management is an ongoing journey. I urge you to continue learning and seeking out resources that enhance your skills. Attend workshops, read widely, and engage in reflective practices. By committing to continuous improvement, you can ensure that your conflict management abilities remain sharp and relevant.

Thank you for taking this journey with me. I am confident that, with dedication and practice, you will transform your workplace into a thriving environment where every voice is heard, and every conflict is an opportunity for growth.

Amber Preston

References

Acrolinx. (2024, August 30). *Empathetic communication: Why is it important at work?* Retrieved from https://www.acrolinx.com/blog/empathetic-communication-why-is-it-important-at-work/

Aurora Training Advantage. (n.d.). *Conflict resolution: A quality found in effective leaders.* Retrieved from https://auroratrainingadvantage.com/leadership/conflict-resolution-leadership-quality/

CA Consumer Law APC. (2023, September 26). *Why neutrality is crucial in mediation.* Retrieved from https://caconsumerlaw.com/blog/why-neutrality-is-crucial-in-mediation/

Coursera. (2024, October 25). *Assertive communication: Definition, examples, and tips.* Retrieved from https://www.coursera.org/articles/assertive-communication

CTR Institute. (n.d.). *10 strategies for dealing with passive-aggressive people.* Retrieved from https://ctrinstitute.com/blog/10-strategies-for-dealing-with-passive-aggressive-people/

Ethics.org. (n.d.). *The PLUS ethical decision making model.* Retrieved from https://www.ethics.org/resources/free-toolkit/decision-making-model/

Euronext. (2025, January 9). *8 steps to develop a strong compliance strategy.* Retrieved from https://www.corporateservices.euronext.com/blog/compliance/strategy

Exude Inc. (2020, July 23). *Positive conflict resolution in remote work environments.* Retrieved from https://www.exudeinc.com/blog/positive-conflict-resolution-in-remote-work-environments/

Forbes Human Resources Council. (2019, November 5). *12 dispute mediation techniques for managers.* Retrieved from https://www.forbes.com/councils/forbeshumanresourcescouncil/2019/11/05/12-dispute-mediation-techniques-for-managers/

Harvard Business Review. (2023, October). *What we get wrong about empathic leadership.* Retrieved from https://hbr.org/2023/10/what-we-get-wrong-about-empathic-leadership

Huthwaite International. (n.d.). *How to master virtual communications: 10 expert tips.* Retrieved from https://www.huthwaiteinternational.com/blog/effective-virtual-communication

Indeed. (2024, November 4). *Active listening in the workplace: How it makes you a better manager.* Retrieved from https://www.indeed.com/hire/c/info/active-listening-in-the-workplace-for-managers

JAMS Pathways. (2024, September 6). *Addressing conflict in a remote setting: Strategies for success*. Retrieved from https://www.jamspathways.com/news-insights/addressing-conflict-in-a-remote-setting-strategies-for-success

JAMS Pathways. (n.d.). *Workplace conflict resolution success stories & case studies*. Retrieved from https://www.jamspathways.com/successstories

Kurter, H. L. (2022, January 27). *3 ways to best handle aggressive people in the workplace*. Retrieved from https://www.forbes.com/sites/heidilynnekurter/2022/01/27/3-ways-to-best-handle-aggressive-people-in-the-workplace/

Law Birdie. (2023, July 30). *Workplace conflict and employment laws*. Retrieved from https://lawbirdie.com/workplace-conflict-and-employment-laws/

LeaderFactor. (2024, October 16). *Psychological safe space*. Retrieved from https://www.leaderfactor.com/learn/psychological-safe-space

Life Coach Training. (n.d.). *The importance of emotional intelligence in conflict resolution*. Retrieved from https://lifecoachtraining.co/the-importance-of-emotional-intelligence-in-conflict-resolution/

Mayo Clinic. (2023, December 23). *Resilience: Build skills to endure hardship*. Retrieved from https://www.mayoclinic.org/tests-procedures/resilience-training/in-depth/resilience/art-20046311

Mediation Training Institute. (n.d.). *Conflict competence*. Retrieved from https://www.mediationworks.com/conflict-competence/

Mind Tools. (n.d.). *8 ways to improve self-regulation - "Feed your good wolf"*. Retrieved from https://www.mindtools.com/aunxs99/8-ways-to-improve-self-regulation

Mind Tools. (n.d.). *Virtual team-building exercises*. Retrieved from https://www.mindtools.com/a3pfy3c/virtual-team-building-exercises

Psychology Today. (2024, March 5). *9 steps for successfully managing conflict with a narcissist*. Retrieved from https://www.psychologytoday.com/us/blog/childhood-narcissism/202403/9-steps-for-successfully-managing-conflict-with-a-narcissist

SHRM. (2024, September 19). *Why HR confidentiality is essential for protecting employees*. Retrieved from https://www.shrm.org/topics-tools/tools/hr-answers/confidentiality-critical-to-human-resources

Siragusa, T. (2023, October 16). *Redefining conflict resolution: The design thinking way*. Retrieved from https://tulliosiragusa.com/resolving-conflict/

Speakeasy. (2024, May 14). *The importance of non-verbal communication skills in conflict resolution*. Retrieved from https://www.speakeasyinc.com/the-importance-of-non-verbal-communication-skills-in-conflict-resolution/

The Collective. (2023, February 20). *Innovate through conflict: A tech leadership guide*. Retrieved from https://www.jointhecollective.com/article/conflict-resolution-and-innovation--turning-disagreements-into-opportunities/

The Maker Group. (n.d.). *Benefits and strategies for a successful win-win negotiation.* Retrieved from https://themakergroup.com/win-win-negotiation/

The Myers-Briggs Company. (2020, March 13). *Myers-Briggs Type Indicator® conflict style report.* Retrieved from https://www.themyersbriggs.com/en-US/Products-and-Services/-/media/myers-briggs/files/sample-reports/smp261161.pdf

Versed. (n.d.). *Uncover conflict roots with five whys.* Retrieved from https://www.versed.uk/blog/uncover-conflict-roots-with-five-whys

Vistage. (2023, May 12). *What are the best negotiation strategies?* Retrieved from https://www.vistage.com/research-center/business-growth-strategy/six-successful-strategies-for-negotiation/

Voltage Control. (2024, February 13). *Navigating conflict and fostering open communication.* Retrieved from https://voltagecontrol.com/articles/navigating-conflict-and-fostering-open-communication-a-collaborative-leadership-approach/

www.ingramcontent.com/pod-product-compliance
Lightning Source LLC
Chambersburg PA
CBHW071340210326
41597CB00015B/1512